Make Your Way To
DESTINY

THE *JOURNEY* FROM JACOB TO ISRAEL

II

Make Your Way To
DESTINY

THE *JOURNEY* FROM JACOB TO ISRAEL

Chudi Egbuonu

Author of 'You can be the next Success Story'

Make Your Way To
DESTINY

THE *JOURNEY* FROM JACOB TO ISRAEL

All Scripture texts, unless otherwise stated, are taken from the New King James Version (NKJV)

ISBN: 978-978-960-709-9

Published by Pastureland Resources
Printed in the Federal Republic of Nigeria

For further information or permission, contact:

Pastureland Resources
E-mail: pasturetonic@yahoo.co.uk,
egbuonu75@gmail.com
Tel: +44 785 891 5070, +234 803 700 8069
+44 792 743 2456

DEDICATION

To all who desire to make the journey of life
on their *purposeway* and to
reach their destiny.

VI

CONTENTS

X

INTRODUCTION

Genesis 32:27-28

27 So He said to him, "What is your name?" He said, "Jacob."

28 And He said, "Your name shall no longer be called Jacob, but Israel; for you have struggled with God and with men, and have prevailed."

Gen 35: 10

10 And God said to him, "Your name is Jacob; your name shall not be called Jacob anymore, but Israel shall be your name." So He called his name Israel.

The very first impression any reader of the Bible will get of Jacob is that of someone that placed a high premium on human efforts. When his mother conceived of him and his brother Esau, we see in Genesis 25:22 that the two brothers jostled each other in their mother's womb. And during their delivery, with Esau coming out before him, Jacob's hand held Esau's heel as he (Jacob) came out.

That led to his been named Jacob. The name

means "He grasps the heel." It paints the picture of a supplanter; a deceiver.

However, when Rebekah inquired of the Lord what the matter was, with the children struggling within her, God told her that she was pregnant with two children who will be the progenitors of two nations. He also told her that these two nations will be hostile to one another, and that the younger child - and by inference, the nation he will father - will be greater and stronger than the older child and his nation.

> **God's people are not the products of natural or worldly development, but of His sovereign predetermination and intervention in the affairs of men.**

God's election of Jacob, therefore, even before he was born, highlights the fact that God's people are not the products of natural or worldly development, but of His sovereign predetermination and intervention in the affairs of men. It showcases the truth that His choices are not predicated on human reasoning or logic, and definitely not on human efforts or input.

Ecclesiastes 9: 11

11 I returned and saw under the sun that –
the race is not to the swift, nor the battle
to the strong, nor bread to the wise,
nor riches to men of understanding, nor
favour to men of skill: but time and
chance happen to them all.

In concluding that "time and chance" happen to all men, the author of Ecclesiastes, most probably King Solomon, in his legendary wisdom, asserted that man did not have the ultimate control or say concerning events or the course of his life. In spite of his having been on the side of advantage of God's election, what we see in Jacob's early life in a resolute determination to influence, by the dynamics of human input, the happenings in, and the direction of his life. However, with his encounters with

God's choices are not predicated on human reasoning or logic, and definitely not on human efforts or input.

God at Peniel (in Genesis 32) and Bethel (in Genesis 35), Jacob experienced a monumental transformation.

With those encounters, Jacob became Israel. The name, Israel, means "God rules". It paints the picture of someone in whose life the purpose of God is evidently on course. He moved from the place of human input and manipulation to the place of God's input and control. He changed from one that was ready to do anything to get his desires, no matter whose ox was gored, to one that saw the will of God as the uppermost consideration in any matter.

Jacob's path to becoming Israel is a story of positive elements of his character because, though he was a supplanter; a cheat; a deceiver, he still manifested a lot of very admirable character traits which played defining roles in this classic march-to-destiny story. Because, his election by God notwithstanding, he still needed to align with God's will to make His (God's) plan and purpose for him real (2 Peter 1:10). So many callings and elections, in and outside Scriptures, have been aborted or miscarried; so many destinies have been destroyed by

> **Many callings and elections have been aborted or miscarried by carelessness or outright misbehaviour.**

the carelessness or outright misbehaviour of the subjects and carriers of such elections and destinies.

People like Samson and King Saul failed to comport themselves as was befitting of their glorious destinies and consequently could not fulfil same. Even Moses, in spite of his outstanding success in delivering the Israelites from bondage in Egypt, was unable to reach his destiny of leading them into Canaan.

> **When purpose is discovered and prosecuted, your walk on your 'purposeway' will ultimately lead you to your destiny.**

Purpose originates from God, our Creator, while man is the one who 'works out' destiny. When purpose is discovered and prosecuted, your walk on your 'purposeway' (the path along which you prosecute God's purpose for you) will ultimately lead you to your destiny. Destiny therefore lies or is located at the end of your purposeway. That is why fulfilment of destiny does not happen in a moment, a month, a year, or even several years, but

> **Destiny lies or is located at the end of your purposeway**

over a lifetime.

It's critical to know that your purposeway cannot be outside God. For you to be truly on your purposeway, you must be in Christ; you must be a member of God's family, since man was made to worship Him. That primary general purpose precedes the specific purpose you, as an individual, were made to accomplish.

Your purposeway cannot be outside God.

God's purpose for creating all things was to bring Him pleasure. "Thou art worthy, O Lord, to receive glory and honour and power: for thou hast created all things, and by thy pleasure they are and were created" (Rev. 4:11, KJV). He made man to worship Him. "When all has been heard, the end of the matter is: fear God (WORSHIP HIM with awe-filled reverence, ..., for THIS APPLIES TO EVERY PERSON" (Eccl. 12:13, AMP).

God called out the church to attract praise to Him. "This people I have formed for myself; they shall declare my praise"(Is. 43:21). Every genuine purpose therefore brings God pleasure, prosecutes worship to Him, and attracts praise to Him.

As you journey on your purposeway to your destiny, your transformation is continuous and progressive. That is to say that transformation is a co-traveller with prosecution of purpose on the way to destiny. The transformation must not be made up of sensational Peniel-like experiences like Jacob had. The important thing is for the way you think to continue to change (becoming more and more like how God thinks), and for that to execute progressive change in you.

> **Every genuine purpose therefore brings God pleasure, prosecutes worship to Him, and attracts praise to Him.**

Notable points in Jacob's interesting story include his purchasing of the birthright of his elder brother, Esau, with a meal of bread and stew of lentils, a sad commentary on Esau's rating of the said birthright. We also see how he, with the prodding and active collaboration of his mother, Rebekah,

> **As you journey on your purposeway to your destiny, your transformation is continuous and progressive.**

deceived his old and almost blind father, Isaac, into bestowing upon him Isaac's final blessing. Thereafter, **Transformation is a co-traveller with prosecution of purpose on the way to destiny** again on his mother's advice, we see him flee from a furious Esau to the house of his maternal uncle, Laban, in Haran. On the way to Haran, he had a memorable encounter with 'the God of his fathers', Abraham and Isaac, at his camp in Bethel.

In Laban's house, he offered to serve his uncle for seven years as a bride price for Rachel, Laban's younger daughter.When he was deceitfully given Leah, Laban's first daughter, as wife, instead of his preferred Rachel, at the end of the seven years, he was made to serve Laban for another seven years in order to marry Rachel. Afterwards, he served as a junior business partner to Laban for another six years.

At the end of twenty years in Haran, he decided to return to his homeland. It was on his way back home that he had the encounters which were critical transformation experiences in his journey to destiny.

My prayer is that your encounter with God through the pages of this book will both provoke and prosecute transformation in your life, and strengthen your walk to your destiny. From now on, your life will no longer be the story of human or satanic manipulation. The control of God over your life will become manifest, in the mighty name of Jesus Christ.

Chapter 1

A PROPER VALUE SYSTEM

Genesis 25: 29- 34

29 Now Jacob cooked a stew; and Esau came in from the field, and he was weary.

30 And Esau said to Jacob, "Please feed me with that same red stew, for I am weary." Therefore his name was called Edom.

31 But Jacob said, "Sell me your birthright as of this day."

32 And Esau said, "Look, I am about to die, so what is this birthright to me?"

33 The Jacob said, "Swear to me as of this day." So he swore to him, and sold his birthright to Jacob.

34 And Jacob gave Esau bread and stew of lentils; then he ate and drank, arose and went his way. Thus Esau despised his birthright.

The above account is a sad but solid commentary on the value systems of the two brothers in question. Esau valued stew more than the birthright, while Jacob valued the birthright more than his integrity. Esau was definitely not "about to die" (Vs. 32). We were not told that he had gone without food (and water) for several days. He probably had even taken breakfast earlier in the morning of that same day before he went out to the field.

He just did not have any iota of regard for his birthright. He saw it as being of not real and practical value. On the contrary, the first medium of exchange that came to Jacob's mind to request from his brother for the food Esau asked from him was Esau's birthright. That suggests to me that he had desired the birthright for some time. He must have secretly wished that he was the firstborn, and the owner of the birthright.

All through Jacob's life, we see this same determination to get what he really desired, even if by foul means. Condemnable as his manners of going for his desires were in his early life, it could hardly be argued that the objects he

Your values control your behaviour. usually craved for were normally things of great value. With his encounter with God, he did away with selfishness and craftiness, and the deficiency these character traits injected into his value system was eliminated. His value system thereafter became more wholesome and proper.

The Cambridge English Dictionary defines values as "the beliefs people have, especially about what is right and wrong and what is most important in life, that control their behaviour." Your values, therefore, control your behaviour. Ultimately, your behaviour plays a role in determining you will be, and what you will have, later in life.

Your behaviour plays a role in determining you will be, and what you will have, later in life.

Mathew 13: 44 – 46 (NIV)

44 The kingdom of heaven is like treasure
    hidden in a field. When a man found
    it, he hid it again, and then in his
    joy went and sold all he had and bought

that field.

45 Again, the kingdom of heaven is like a merchant looking for fine pearls.

46 When he found one of GREAT VALUE, he went away and sold EVERYTHING he had and bought it.

The extent to which you value a thing determines the extent to which you will go to get it. It's the value you place on a thing that produces your behaviour with regards to it. Though speaking in a parable, Jesus' message was unambiguous. He meant that whoever truly desired to spend eternity in God's presence will do everything that is needed to make that happen.

Your values are a highway to your make-up and habitat in the future.

Your values are a highway to your make-up and habitat in the future. They determine the destination to which you are headed – who and where you will be later in life. Everybody gets transformed, with the passage of time, in accordance with the values he/she had earlier in life.

Romans 12:2 (NLT)

2 Don't copy the behaviour and customs of this world, but let God transform you into a new person by changing the way you think. Then you will learn to know God's will for you, which is good and pleasing and perfect.

When you allow God to transform you, you become the new person He wants you to be. When you let God's word and will to transform you, you become who He created you to be. It is therefore critical to have or to cultivate the right values, seeing that values situate or control behaviour, and behaviour helps to make who you become.

> **Everybody gets transformed, with the passage of time, in accordance with the values he/she had earlier in life.**

LEARN TO UPHOLD KINGDOM VALUES

There are values that are generally accepted and cherished by just about everyone. Values such as honesty, integrity, trust, dedication and consistency resonate with virtually every person or group of persons. Specifically however, every community, group, organisation, etc., has values it specially promotes, accepts and rewards. This is very true of the kingdom of God.

Aside from the generally accepted ones earlier mentioned, core values in the kingdom of God include holiness, soul winning, fellowship, generosity, prayerfulness, faith, forgiveness, knowledge and vision. The nine attributes of the Christian life/character, which Paul called the fruit of the Holy Spirit, in Galatians 5:22-23 - love, joy, peace, patience, kindness, goodness, faithfulness, gentleness, and self-control (NLT), are very much values in the kingdom of God.

Matthew 6:33

33 But seek first the kingdom of God and His righteousness, and all these things shall be added to you.

As a believer; as a citizen of God's kingdom, God wants you to get your priorities right. Your value system must reflect the kingdom to which you belong. Your number one priority should be God's kingdom and His righteousness. The Amplified Version of the Bible says "His righteousness", in Matthew 6:33, is "His way of doing and being right – the attitude and character of

Your value system must reflect the kingdom to which you belong.

God." Of course, the attitude and character of God denote God's behaviour.

As we have seen from its definition, values control behaviour. If your values, therefore, are godly, your behaviour will also be godly. If your values are God's kingdom-related, your behaviour will also be His kingdom-compliant.

Some of the things we have heard and read about a number of 'God's Generals' of yester-years are a glowing tribute to how kingdom values occupied pole positions in their hearts. John Wesley said, "Let us all be of one business. We live only for this, to save our own souls and the souls of those who hear us." John Knox prayed all-night in agonising tones, "Lord, give me Scotland or I die." David Brainard, a missionary to American Indians, wrote, "I cared not where or how I lived or what hardships I went through so that I could gain souls for Christ."

George Whitefield, a great evangelist and friend of John Wesley, prayed, "O Lord, give me souls or take my soul." William Booth, founder of the Salvation Army was asked by the king of England what the ruling force in his life was. He replied, "Sir, some men's passion is for gold; other men's passion is for fame, but my passion is for souls."

St. Patrick, a rugged believer who was said to have brought even dead animals and trees back to life, prayed, "God give me souls or give me nothing else." Brethren during the Hebrides Revival of 1949-1952 prayed, "Lord, if you will not use us, please, kill us." The brethren from England who brought the 'fire' from Azusa Street Revival to England gathered everyday under the terrible cold. Their only prayer topic was, "Lord, give us men that will spread your fire in the streets of England."

During the Indonesian Revival, the people's prayer by day and night was, "Lord, the harvest is ripe. If it pleases you, please use us." William Seymour's usual prayer was, "Lord, this is another day that hell must lose men and women. Please, we are here. Use us."

Little wonder therefore, that God used these men and women greatly. They served and impacted their generations. As I was writing this book, I received a message from a pastor friend via WhatsApp that spoke to how improper the values of believers had become.

"Isn't it strange how N500 seems like such a large amount when we give it as offering, but such a small amount when you go shopping?

"Isn't it strange how two hours seem so long when you're in church to worship God, but how short they seem when you're watching a good movie?

"Isn't it strange that you can't find a word to say when you're making supplication to God, but you've no trouble thinking of what to gist about with a friend?

"Isn't it strange how difficult and boring it is to read one chapter of the Scriptures, but how easy it is to read 100 pages of a popular novel/ magazine?

"Isn't it strange how everyone wants front-row tickets to concerts, movies or games, but they do whatever is possible to sit on the last row in a church service?

"Isn't it strange how everyone wants a place in heaven, but they don't want to believe, do or say anything to get there?

"Isn't it strange how we send jokes in e-mails, BBM, WhatsApp, etc., and they are forwarded immediately, but when we are going to share messages about God, we think about it twice?

"IT'S STRANGE; ISN'T IT?"

Matthew 6:19-21

19 Do not lay up for yourselves treasures on earth, where moth and rust destroy and where thieves break in and steal;

20 but lay up for yourselves treasures in heaven, where neither moth nor rust destroys and where thieves do not break in and steal.

21 FOR WHERE YOUR TREASURE IS, THERE YOUR HEART WILL BE ALSO

Your treasure is that which is precious to you. It is what is of great value to you. Jesus said the 'location' of whatever is precious to you automatically becomes the 'location' of your heart. Obviously, the reverse is also true. The 'location' of your heart announces the 'location' of one or more things that are of great value to you.

This is to say that your treasure and your heart will always 'dwell together.' Let's not deceive ourselves. If you truly love or value something or someone, you will invest your time, money, energy, etc. in that thing or person. If, therefore, there's no push or pull on your inside towards investing your time, money or energy in something or someone, you can be sure that you do not have significant love or value for that thing.

> **The 'location' of whatever is precious to you automatically becomes the 'location' of your heart.**

However, love or value for a person or thing can be cultivated or developed. We saw earlier that God can "transform you into a new person by changing the way you think" (Romans 12:2, NLT). The New King James Version puts it this way, "... be transformed by the renewing of your mind." You can get your mind renewed by the intake and deliberate practice of the Word of God.

The way to cultivate or develop love or value for someone or something is to consciously and deliberately begin to invest in that person or thing even without having any affection or value for him/her or it. Sooner or later, you will begin to love and value that person or thing.

Matthew 5:44

44 But I say to you, LOVE your enemies, bless those who curse you, DO GOOD to those who hate you, and PRAY for those who spitefully use you and persecute you.

Jesus was saying that the way to love was to do good and to pray. Since to pray is good, Jesus was saying that to act lovingly is to do good. Jesus was not commanding His listener (and us) to feel love. Feelings cannot be commanded but actions can certainly be commanded.

When you act love, very soon you will begin to feel love. That is to say that loving actions beget loving feeling. A number of marriages, for example, have resulted from men and women (who didn't feel love for one another) spending time together, exchanging gifts and so on, and with time, starting to feel love for themselves.

When you act love, very soon you will begin to feel love.

You can, therefore, cultivate or develop love or value for the kingdom of God and God's ways of doing things. You can do that by investing your valuable resources - your time, money, talent, etc. – in His kingdom and His ways of doing things, even when you do not as yet have the corresponding love or value for them. When you do so persistently, over time, you will definitely begin to love and value the kingdom and God's ways of doing things.

Loving actions beget loving feeling.

Like Jesus said in Matthew 6:21, your treasure and your heart will always co-habit. Therefore, when you 'send' the resources you value to a particular 'location,' your heart will, without fail, go there. When you 'send' your treasures to the kingdom of God, your heart will

When you 'send' the resources you value to a particular 'location,' your heart will, without fail, go there.

also go there. That is one way to develop and cultivate kingdom values.

THE DIFFERENCE BETWEEN JACOB AND ESAU

The difference between Jacob and Esau was that Jacob valued spiritual riches while Esau did not. Actually, the Bible says he despised his birthright (Genesis 25:34), a very critical spiritual treasure. Jacob was concerned with the future, while Esau cared only about the immediate present.

The difference between Jacob and Esau was that Jacob valued spiritual riches while Esau did not.

Jacob was a man of vision, while Esau lacked vision.

Hebrew 12: 16-17 (NLT)

16 Make sure that no one is immoral or

godless like Esau, who traded his birthright as the firstborn son for a single meal.

17 You know that AFTERWARD, when he wanted his father's blessing, he was rejected. It was too late for repentance, even though he begged with bitter tears.

At the time he sold his birthright, Esau did not reckon with the 'afterward'. That is one of the core attributes of carnality – not reckoning with the 'afterward.' Carnality has to do with upholding values which are inspired by the flesh, while spirituality is about upholding values which are inspired by the Holy Spirit. To be carnal is to 'sow' to the flesh, that is to invest as directed by the flesh, while spirituality is to invest as directed by the Holy Spirit.

At the time he sold his birthright, Esau did not reckon with the 'afterward'.

Galatians 6:7-9

7 Do not be deceived, God is not mocked; for whatever a man sows, that he will

also reap.

8   For he who sows to his flesh will of the flesh reap corruption, but he who sows to the Spirit will of the Spirit reap everlasting life.

9   And let us not grow weary while doing good, for in due season we shall reap if we do not lose heart.

The flesh does not only refer to the physical body but also to learned independence from God. It is the tendency to act independent of God, acquired outside of our relationship with God. When you continue to invest as directed by the Holy Spirit by doing good, that is by upholding godly values; by behaving well, in due time, you will receive God's reward. Esau was given to investing as directed by the flesh, and in due time, or 'afterward,' he received the reward of the flesh. He certainly did not factor in the 'afterward' when behaving like he did.

One of the core attributes of carnality is not reckoning with the 'afterward'.

When you are flesh-driven, your values will be

such like have only earthly relevance and reward. Another way to put it is that your values will only profit you in the 'here-and-now.' But, when you are Spirit-driven, your values will be such

> **When you are flesh-driven, your values will be such like have only earthly relevance and reward.**

as have both earthly and heavenly relevance and reward.

Mark 8:36

36 For what will it profit a man if he gains the whole world, and loses his own soul?

1Timothy 4:8

8 ..., but godliness is profitable for all things, having promise of the life that now is and of that which is to come.

Jacob, unlike Esau, was always concerned with the 'afterward'. He bought the birthright, with his eyes fixed firmly on the 'afterward'. He served his uncle, Laban, for twenty years, with his eyes on the 'afterward'. He refused to let go of God at Peniel (Genesis 32:26), with his eyes on the 'afterward'.

Foresight is the ability to see a sufficient part of tomorrow (i.e. the future) in order to act appropriately today (i.e. the present). In every pursuit in life, foresight puts you in a vantage position to make profit; to access increase. Vision is foresight with insight, having confidence on (God's) oversight. It is seeing the future as a consequence of your understanding of God's plan and purpose for your life, being confident that God is watching over you as you move in that direction, According to Dr. Paul Eneche, "Life without a bearing is a burden." Bearing, of course, is a component of vision.

Foresight is the ability to see a sufficient part of tomorrow in order to act appropriately today.

Looking at all of Jacob's life, his interest in the covenant God established with his grandfather, Abraham, was clear and unmistakeable. He was committed to seeing the promises contained in that covenant fulfilled. He positioned himself and his family, nuclear and extended, to truly be the heirs to those promises,

Vision is foresight with insight, having confidence on (God's) oversight.

in part, where possible, during his lifetime, and much more wholesomely, after his lifetime. In response to Jacob's value for spiritual riches, God appeared to him at Bethel, and affirmed him to be the custodian of the Abrahamic covenant.

Genesis 28:13-15

13 And behold, the LORD stood above it and
    said: "I am the LORD God of Abraham
    your father and the God of Isaac;
    the land on which you lie I will give to you
    and your descendants.

14 "Also your descendants shall be as the
    dust of the earth; you shall spread
    abroad to the west and the east, to
    the north and the south; and in
    you and in your seed all the families
    of the earth shall be blessed.

15 "Behold, I am with you and will keep you
    wherever you go, and will bring you back
    to this land; for I will not leave you until
    I have done what I have spoken to you."

When your value system is proper, God will cause you to experience transformation. It does not matter how far you go or are taken away from God's 'land' for you.If only you can cultivate and uphold the values of God's kingdom, God will bring you back to His 'land' for you. He will not leave you until He has completed what He has declared concerning you.

When your value system is proper, God will cause you to experience transformation.

Chapter 2

A SOLID PARTNERSHIP WITH GOD

Genesis 28: 20-22

20 Then Jacob made a vow, saying, "If God will be with me, and keep me in this way that I am going, and give me bread to eat and clothing to put on,

21 "so that I come back to my father's house in peace, then the LORD shall be my God.

22 "And this stone which I have set as a pillar shall be God's house, and of all that You give me I will surely give a tenth to You."

The initiative to establish a partnership with God was Jacob's. It was not an instruction by God to him. Of course, he may have been told by his father, Isaac, that his grandfather, Abraham, was a tither, as seen in Genesis 14:20. His parents, Isaac and Rebekah, had probably taught him how important God was to his financial prosperity, and, therefore, how he should learn to heed God's instructions with regards to the management of his finances. Isaac must have told him the story of how God instructed him to remain in Gerar, and not to go down to Egypt, during famine, and how he obeyed, and that when he sowed in that land (Gerar), he reaped a hundredfold the same year (Genesis 26: 1-2, 12).

However, it was still to Jacob's credit that, in the absence of his parents, as he (Jacob) was on the way to the house of his uncle, Laban, in Padam Aram, on perceiving the presence of God in Luz (which Jacob then named Bethel), he immediately entered into a partnership with God. He vowed to give back to God ten percent of all that God blessed him with, if God would be with him on his journey and brought him back to his father's house in peace. That translated to giving God ten percent of whatever financial and material increase God blessed him with after that encounter.

Jacob's decision to enter into a partnership with God is even more impressive considering the age at which he did this. Jacob was probably seventy-seven years old at this time. To get this, you will have to fast-forward to when he and his other children went over from Canaan to Egypt on his son, Joseph's invitation. Jacob was one hundred and thirty years old then (Genesis 47:9).

We can see that Joseph was thirty nine years old at that time, since he was thirty when he interpreted Pharaoh's dreams and Pharaoh made him his (Pharaoh's) deputy (Genesis 41:46), and that he had superintended over the affairs of Egypt for the seven years of abundance and two years of famine by the time his family came to join him. Subtracting thirty-nine from one hundred and thirty, you get ninety-one. Jacob was therefore ninety-one years old when Joseph was born.

We also know that Jacob had served his uncle, Laban, for fourteen years by the time Joseph was born (Genesis 30:25), and served him a further six years before he left Padan Aram, bringing his total years of service to twenty (Genesis 31:41). When you subtract fourteen from ninety-one, you get seventy-seven. Jacob was therefore seventy-seven years old at the time he left his parents' home for his uncle's house in Padan Aram and ninety-seven when he left Padan Aram to return home. It was at seventy-seven, on the way to Padan Aram that he met with God, and entered into a partnership with Him.

The wisdom of entering into this partnership, and of God's approval of the same, are evident in Jacob's words to his wives, Rachel and Leah, shortly before he left Padan Aram.

Genesis 31: 4-13

4   So Jacob sent and called Rachel and Leah to the field to his flock,

5   And said to them, "I see your father's countenance, that it is not favourable toward me as before; but the God of my father has been with me.

6   "And you know that with all my might I have served your father.

7   "Yet your father has deceived me and changed my wages ten times, but God did not allow him to hurt me.

8   "If he said thus: 'The speckled shall be your wages,' then all the flocks

bore speckled. And if he said thus:
'The streaked shall be your wages,'
then all the flocks bore streaked.

9 "So God has taken away the livestock of
your father and given them to me.

10 "And it happened, at the time when the
flocks conceived, that I lifted my eyes
and saw in a dream, and behold the
rams which leaped upon
the flocks were streaked, speckled,
and gray-spotted.

11 "Then the Angel of God spoke to me in a
dream, saying, 'Jacob.' And I said,
'Here I am.'

12 "And He said, Lift your eyes now and
see, all the rams which leap on the
flocks are streaked, speckled, and
gray-spotted; for I have seen all
that Laban is doing to you.

13 'I AM THE GOD OF BETHEL, where you
anointed the pillar and WHERE YOU
MADE A VOW TO ME. Now arise, get out
of this land, and return to the land of
your family.' "

In that 'meeting' with his wives, Rachel and Leah, Jacob succinctly enumerated some of the benefits he had enjoyed so far from the partnership that he entered into with God twenty years earlier. He said he had enjoyed God's presence, even with Laban's unfavourable attitude towards him (Vs. 5), God's protection (Vs.7), and abundant prosperity, even with Laban's regular changing of the terms of their partnership (Vs.7) and Laban's deceptions. He told them that the reality of the day was that all the 'quality livestock,' i.e. "the rams which leaped" (Vs. 10, 12), at the time he was talking, belonged to him (Jacob).

The partnership Jacob had with God catapulted him from a run-away with next to nothing to a man that was "exceedingly prosperous, and had large flocks, female and male servants, and camels and donkeys" (Genesis 30:43). It promoted him from one that left his father's house with just a staff (i.e. a stick) to one that had two companies of

The partnership Jacob had with God catapulted him from a run-away with next to nothing to a man that was exceedingly prosperous.

people and animals by the time he was returning twenty years later (Genesis 32:7, 10). His was indeed an amazing story of transformation.

POWERED BY PRINCIPLES

A principle is a fundamental truth or proposition on which a system of belief or chain of reasoning rests. According to the Cambridge English Dictionary, it is a basic idea or rule that explains or controls how something happens or works. From this definition, you can see that personal success in life is largely a function of compliance with, or adherence to divine principles. It is also deduceable from the

> **While laws are usually temporary and changeable, divine principles are eternal and unchangeable.**

definition that laws are products of principles. That is to say that it is principles that give birth to laws.

However, while laws are usually temporary (i.e. time-configured) and changeable, divine principles are eternal (i.e. timeless) and unchangeable. And so, the abrogation of a law does not translate to the demise (i.e. death) or annulment of the principles from which the law was enacted. All through the dispensations in which man has lived, from the Dispensation of Innocence, in which Adam and Eve lived (Genesis 1), to that of Conscience, in which Noah lived (Genesis 6), to that of Human Government, with the Tower of Babel (Genesis 11), to that of Promise, in which Abraham lived (Genesis 12), to that of the Law, in which Moses lived (Exodus 20), to that of Grace, which Jesus' death and resurrection ushered us into, while laws have been enacted and abolished, divine principles have remained the same.

> **The abrogation of a law does not translate to the demise or annulment of the principles from which the law was enacted.**

One of the major principles in the kingdom of God is the principles of provision. This principle requires us to give before we receive. The principle says that when we put God first in our lives, He is faithful to meet our needs. The principle also works to the end that when you willingly make available to God what you have for the benefit of His kingdom. He will bless you to the extent that you will not have sufficient space to store the blessing.

We see the operation of this principle in Luke 5:1-11. After Jesus had made use of Simon's boat, obviously with Simon's permission, to teach the multitude, Jesus asked Simon to launch out into the deep and let down his nets to catch fish. Even though Simon and his colleagues had earlier failed to catch any fish throughout the night, which was a far better time to fish, he obeyed Jesus and amazingly he and his colleagues "caught a great number of fish, and their net was breaking" (Luke 5:6). Other Scriptures which attest to the potency of the principle of provision are Matthew 6:33, 2 Corinthians 9:6-7 and Luke 6:38.

When you look at all the laws from Exodus to Deuteronomy, you see the principles behind them. For example, the law in Deuteronomy 22:5 that a woman must not wear men's clothes and vice-versa was derived from the principle of decency. The abrogation of the law was not the abrogation of the principle.

The law in Deuteronomy 25:13 forbidding a person from having two different weights in his/her bag was derived from the principle of honesty. Again, the abrogation of the law did not equate the abrogation of the principle. The law in Deuteronomy 22:8 that whoever built a new house must make a parapet around the roof to prevent people from falling from the roof was derived from the principle of being your brother's keeper and the principle of safety. The abrogation of that law was not also the annulment of the principles which birthed it.

Embodied in the principle of provision is the principle of partnering with God to advance His kingdom/interests. The number one reason, arguably, for lack and want; for insufficiency; for poverty amongst Christians is the non-adherence to this principle. If you are to go beyond financial and material barriers and attain unto the financial and material heights God has in mind for you, then you must become a significant investor in God's kingdom.

Outside of that, of course, you can still prosper financially. You can still have your needs met a lot of time as you think hard, work hard, etc., but you will fall many miles short of your destiny, not just financially and materially, but in other facets of life.

Luke 16:11

11 Therefore if you have not been faithful in the righteous mammon, who will commit to your trust the true riches?

As a child of God, a very important aspect of faithfulness with money is giving to God through His church. The New Living Translation (NLT) renders "unrighteous mammon" as "worldly wealth." To be faithful with your wealth - financial and material - is to use or manage same properly. To do so is to distribute your wealth equitably, with God, you, your loved ones, and other people and matters getting their "fair shares."

If truly God is your Partner, then you must ensure that you give Him His fair share of the money that comes to you at all times.

If truly God is your Partner, then you must ensure that you give Him His fair share of the money that comes to you at all times. Giving to God, through the church, is done in two basic ways: tithes and offerings (of money). However, you can also give lands, houses, cars and other material possessions, so long as the goal of your giving is the expansion of God's kingdom.

God's greatest heartbeat is the expansion of His kingdom on the earth. God is therefore committed to transforming people who invest wholeheartedly and sacrificially towards this cause. Like He did for Jacob, God makes such people exceedingly prosperous.

Kingdom prosperity is founded on the eternal principle of sowing and reaping (Gen. 8:22). God's greatest demonstration of love was in the giving of His one and only Son, Jesus Christ, to die a shameful death for us. Since He did that, God

Without the seed; without the beginning, you cannot have the next step, not to talk about having the end.

has been reaping millions upon millions of sons (and daughters) because of the infallibility of the law/principle of sowing and reaping. God's demonstration of love also tells us that though it is possible to give without loving, it is not possible to love without giving.

It is important that you understand the power of the seed. The seed is the beginning; the starting point. Without the seed; without the beginning, you cannot have the next step, not to talk about having the end. With vegetation, the seed is therefore of strategic importance, indeed of greater strategic importance than every other part of the plant because it is what determines the continuity or otherwise (i.e. termination) of the lifeline of the plant.

The seed evidences the potential for the manifestation of a forest.

The seed evidences the potential for the manifestation of a tree, and the tree evidences the potential for the manifestation of a forest. You can therefore say that the seed actually evidences the potential for the manifestation of a forest. Put another way, the seed is the bridge or the gateway to the prepared place of a forest.

If you want to know how a man's life will look in the future, find out the seeds he is doing today. This is applicable to every department of life: "… whatever a man sows, that he will also reap" (Gal. 6:7). Financially, for example, a man's financial look in the future (which starts now) will be a product of what and how he sows financially today. It will not depend on his desires, neither will it depend on his needs. Harvest does not answer to desires or needs, but to seeds.

2 Corinthians 9:10

10 Now may He who supplies seed to the sower, and bread for food, supply and multiply the seed you have sown and increase the fruits of your righteousness.

1 Corinthians 15:37-38

37 And what you sow, you do not sow that body that shall be, but mere grain, perhaps wheat or some other grain.

38 But God gives it a body as He pleases,
and to each seed its own body.

Whatever is the desire that you have, what God will do for you is to supply seed to you. When **The divine order is seedtime before harvest.** you sow it, He will then multiply it and give it its body as it pleases Him. When you have a finance-related desire, and have appropriately sown the financial seed God supplied you, He will give the seed its body. You will reap and celebrate a financial harvest.

The divine order is seedtime before harvest. "Most assuredly, I say to you, unless a grain of wheat falls into the ground and dies, it remains alone; but if it dies, it produces much grain" **If you misuse the delivered seed, you will miss out on your desired harvest.** (Jn. 12:24). The sown seed is potent. On the flip side, if you misuse the delivered seed, you will miss out on your desired harvest.

THE TRANSFORMING PRINCIPLE OF TITHING

There are two basic dimensions to open heavens. There is the love/mercy dimension that everyone (and indeed every living creature) enjoys (Mtt. 5:44-45) and there is the kingdom/covenant dimension that every child of God should walk under (Ez. 34:26; Mal. 3:10). There are, however, some key principles that have to be in operation for the heavens to be opened to a kingdom/ covenant magnitude.

For you to enjoy the kingdom/covenant dimension of open heavens, you must be a regular tither and a generous giver of offerings (Gen. 8:22; Mal. 3:8-10). Covenant financial/material harvest answers principally to its kind, i.e. financial/ material seedtime (Gen. 1:11-12). As you exercise and excel in the grace of giving, you will enjoy open heavens.

Tithing is a timeless principle. It began over four hundred years before the law was given (Gen. 14:20); Jesus agreed with it (Mtt. 23:23), and Jesus is our "great High Priest" (Heb. 4:14) whose

The critical issue in tithing is how your heart 'beats'.

priesthood is "in the order of Melchizedek, not in the order of Aaron" (Heb. 7:11, NIV). It is the 'product' of the recognition and acknowledgement of God as (i) Most High, (ii) Creator of heaven and earth, (iii) deserving of praise, and (iv) the Deliverer of your enemies into your hand (Gen. 14: 19-20). Melchizedek declared these truths, and accepting, Abraham "gave him a tithe of all" (Vs. 20).

The critical issue in tithing, as in with giving of any kind, is how your heart 'beats' (Mtt. 6:21). If the kingdom of God (and its advancement) is your heartbeat, you will take pleasure in tithing. If, however, self-centeredness and wealth accumulation are your heartbeat, then you will come up with all kinds of reasons and arguments not to tithe. The love of money is not only in operation when there is the readiness to do anything to get money; it is also in manifestation when there is a strong unwillingness to part with money.

The love of money is not only in operation when there is the readiness to do anything to get money; it is also in manifestation when there is a strong unwillingness to part with money.

The most common argument people put up against tithing is easily the one that it belongs to the Mosaic Law, and passed away with it. This is in spite of the truth that tithing predates the law, as earlier stated. Tithing, therefore, was

Tithing was not <u>only</u> in the law, but was <u>also</u> in the law.

not <u>only</u> in the law, but was <u>also</u> in the law. That is to say that tithing transcends the law. The principle of tithing is embodied in the principle of partnering with God to advance His kingdom.

It is critical to understand that there is a difference between tithing under the Mosaic Covenant and tithing under the New Covenant of Grace. Now, we do not tithe as a matter of law but as a matter of worship (Heb. 7:8). Also, we no longer tithe to the priest, but to Christ. In tithing to the church, the body of Christ, we are tithing to Christ.

Spiritually speaking, there are two kinds of law: the law of the Spirit of life in Christ Jesus and the law of sin and death (Rom. 8:2). The newer explains the older. Freedom from the older demands a fitting into the newer.

We must also know that there is the need for the righteous requirement to be fully met in us (Rom. 8:4). The law remains a moral and ethical guide, even though it is no longer the channel for (spiritual) salvation. The righteous elements of the law should now be obeyed out of love for God and the enabling of His Spirit.

Tithing is actually what you could call a principle of responsible Christianity. When you tithe, you are being principled and not being legalistic. It is comparable to the principle of good/responsible fatherhood. Even though there is perhaps no law in any nation's constitution that says a father must provide for his children, the principle of responsible fatherhood/ parenthood demands it.

Tithing is what you could call a principle of responsible Christianity. When you tithe, you are being principled and not being legalistic.

The practice of responsible fatherhood involves the provision of food, clothing, housing and education for the children. A father can choose to do more, like take the children abroad for holidays, but that is not a requirement for responsible fatherhood. In the same way, a believer can give more than ten percent of what he gets to God but ten percent is the required minimum of the principle of tithing.

Malachi 3:1

1   Behold, I send My messenger, And he
    will prepare the way before Me. And the
    Lord, whom you seek, will suddenly come
    to His temple, even the Messenger of the
    covenant, in whom you delight.
    Behold, He is coming, says
    the Lord of hosts.

Malachi 3:1 foresees the coming of John the Baptist. In that way, that verse and the ones that follow which talk about tithes and offerings are messianic in their postulations.

Malachi 3:8-10

8   Will a man rob God? Yet you have robbed
    Me. But you say, 'In what way have we
    robbed You?' In tithes and offerings.

9   You are cursed with a curse, for you have
    robbed Me, even this whole nation.

10 Bring all the tithes into the storehouse,
   that there may be food in My house,
   and try Me now in this, says the Lord of
   hosts, if I will not open for you the
   windows of heaven and pour out for
   you such blessing that there
   will not be room enough to receive it.

From Mal. 3:8-10, it could be inferred that your level/degree of receipt is determined by your offering, not your tithe. However, it is your tithe that opens the heavens (to a covenant dimension) for God's release to you from heaven to come down. It can be argued, therefore, that without your tithe, the covenant dimension of your release from heaven may not come down, no matter your offering, unless, of course, your offerings from a financial/material blessing exceed ten percent.

In his thoroughly expository book, 'Rediscovering the Kingdom,' Dr. Myles Munroe discussed the concept of kingdom. He submitted that all kingdoms, including the kingdom of God, had certain characteristics and were comprised of a number of components which make for their effective functioning. Two of the characteristics he said all kingdoms had were: Law, i.e. acceptable principles, and A Commonwealth, i.e. economic security.

He enumerated the components all kingdoms were comprised of and what these were in the kingdom of God. Two of these were: A Taxation System (Tithing, in the kingdom of God), and An Economy (a system of Giving and Receiving: seed time and harvest time, in the kingdom of God).

You must understand that as a child of God, you belong to a kingdom – the kingdom of God. Until you begin to view the body of Christ from a kingdom standpoint, your understanding of it will be grossly inadequate. Tithing is the taxation system of the kingdom of God, and its economy is a system of giving and receiving.

> **The surest way to access your prosperity desires is to accede to God's covenant demands.**

Incidentally, many people, who don't believe in giving, believe in receiving. They don't want to sow, but they want to reap. They loathe being involved in seeding, yet they love harvesting. It is, therefore, easy to see that the arguments such people put up against any form of giving (tithing inclusive) are nothing but smokescreens to cover their love of money.

> **The covenant is the conveyor of heaven's best, and the covering against the earth's worst.**

Until you begin to partner with God with your wealth to advance His Kingdom, you should not expect Him to give your efforts to advance financially and materially His full backing. The surest way to access your prosperity desires is to accede to God's covenant demands.

> **kingdom prosperity is more for increase in giving level than it is for improvement in living standard**

The covenant is the conveyor of heaven's best, and the covering against the earth's worst.

We must also know that kingdom prosperity is more for increase in giving level than it is for improvement in living standard (2 Cor. 9:10-11; 2 Cor. 8:7, 13-14). Like the apostle, Paul, also said, "And remember the words of the Lord Jesus, that He said, 'It is MORE BLESSED to give than to receive' (Acts 20:35). This means that giving empowers one to prosper more than receiving does.

The super-giving God wants His children to be great givers. He wants you to partner with Him to advance His kingdom. He wants you to give your tithes regularly and your offerings bountifully in order to enjoy His best for you. He wants you to walk under open heavens at all times. When there is a solid partnership between you and God, you are certainly on your way to transformation, and to your destiny.

Chapter 3

AN UNDERSTANDING OF THE POWER OF VISION

Genesis 30: 29-43

29 So Jacob said to him, "You know how
I have served you and how your livestock
has been with me.

30 "For what you had before I came was
little, and it has increased to a great
amount; the LORD has blessed you
since my coming. And now when
shall I also provide for my own house?"

31 So he said, "What shall I give you?"
And Jacob said, "You shall not give me
anything. If you will do this thing for me,
I will again feed and keep your flocks.

32 "Let me pass through all your flock today,
removing from there all the speckled and
spotted sheep, and all the brown ones
among the lambs, and the spotted and
speckled among the goats; and these
shall be my wages.

33 "So my righteousness will answer for me

in time to come, when the subject of my wages comes before you: every one that is not speckled and spotted among the goats, and brown among the lambs, will be considered stolen, if it is with me."

34 And Laban said, "Oh, that it were according to your word."

35 So he removed that day the male goats that were speckled and spotted, all the female goats that were speckled and spotted, every one that had some white in it, and all the brown ones among the lambs, and gave them into the hand of his sons.

36 The he put three days' journey between himself and Jacob, and Jacob fed the rest of Laban's flocks.

37 Now Jacob took for himself rods of green poplar and of the almond and chestnut trees, peeled white strips in them, and exposed the white which was in the rods.

38 And the rods which he had peeled, he set before the flocks in the gutters, in the

watering troughs where the flocks came to drink, so that they should conceive when they came to drink.

39 So the flocks conceived before the rods, and the flocks brought forth streaked, speckled and spotted.

40 Then Jacob separated the lambs, and made the flocks face towards the streaked and all the brown in the flock of Laban; but he put his own flocks by themselves and did not put them with Laban's flock.

41 And it came to pass, whenever the stronger livestock conceived, that Jacob placed the rods before the eyes of the livestock in the gutters that they might conceive among the rods.

42 But when the flocks were feeble, he did not put them in; so the feebler were Laban's and the stronger Jacob's.

43 Thus the man became exceedingly prosperous, and had large flocks, female and male servants, and camels and donkeys.

From Verse 43, we see that Jacob's becoming exceedingly prosperous was a product of how he put to use his understanding of the power of vision. The first word in that verse, "Thus", makes that clear. In stating his terms for accepting to continue to oversee Laban's flocks, Jacob made propositions which Laban saw as very favourable to him (Laban). In fact, in view of the seemingly disadvantaged position that the terms Jacob proposed placed him (Jacob) in, Laban must have thought Jacob was a fool.

Actually, viewed at the surface, the propositions did seem to be heavily in favour of Laban. What percentage of sheep was speckled and spotted? What percentage of lambs was brown? And, what percentage of goats was speckled and spotted? Obviously, very small. Laban must have been really surprised therefore, indeed shocked, that Jacob proposed that the animals with these features would, from then on, be his (Jacob's) wages in the new arrangement between the two of them.

Little wonder, Laban accepted the terms immediately. He must have seen this new arrangement, a partnership, to be even better for him than the previous one in which he paid Jacob wages. As it turned out, there was something that Jacob knew that Laban did not.

In spite of the advantaged position he perceived himself to already have from Jacob's propositions, Laban still went ahead to remove from his flocks the male goats that were speckled and spotted, all the female goats that were speckled and spotted, every one that had some white in it, and all the brown ones among the lambs (Verse 35). He gave them to his sons. That way, Laban left Jacob without any 'capital' to build on, as far as he (Laban) was concerned.

What Jacob knew that Laban did not was that the critical factor in multiplication or expansion was vision. God said to Abram, "… all the land which you SEE I give to you and your descendants forever" (Gen. 13:15). Evidently, since Abram could not have seen beyond the horizon with his physical eyes, God was talking about what Abram could envision; what he could see with the eyes of his mind. God was talking about what Abram could imagine. Generally speaking still, sight is powerful.

Genesis 15:5-6

5   Then He brought him outside and said,
    "Look now toward heaven, and count the
    stars if you are able to number them."
    And he said to him,
    "So shall your descendants be."

6   And he believed in the LORD,
    and He accounted it to him for
    righteousness.

God helped Abram to believe that he (Abram) was going to be a father of multitudes by showing Abram the numerous stars in heaven. And so, the spoken promise of God to Abram in Genesis 12:1-3 was followed by a divine picture. What you see is critical to what you believe. The seeing could be with your physical eyes or with the eyes of your mind. Somebody said that whatever you fix your eyes on grows within you, and whatever grows within you, you eventually become.

2 Corinthians 5:7

7   For we walk by faith, not by sight.

This is to say that faith is the opposite of sight. However, sight here speaks of the five senses - the seeing, the hearing, the smelling, the touching, and the tasting. As believers, we "LIVE by faith" (as the NIV renders it), not according to the dictates of our five senses.

Since faith is the opposite of sight, and, in practical terms, blindness is also the opposite of sight, we could put the New International Version of 2 Cor. 5:7 this way, "For we live by being blind, not by sight," and the New Living Translation, "For we live by being blind and not by seeing." Actually, living by faith is living by being blind to the suggestions of the five senses, when they run contrary to the word of God. That is because faith is simply agreeing with the word of God, i.e. seeing things the way God sees them. Really, in a manner of speaking, the most important ingredient in faith is sight – God's kind of sight.

2 Corinthians 5:7 (AMP)

7   For we walk by faith, not by sight
    (living our lives in a manner consistent
    with our confident belief in
    God's promises).

Strictly speaking, belief and faith do not mean the same thing. They are however two sides of the same coin. Belief is a state of the heart while faith is the corresponding action to that state. Therefore, faith is acting on what you believe.

No wonder, the Bible says faith without works is dead (James 2:17, 26). This is to say that faith can only be correctly so called if there is an action involved. Faith is an action word. Without action, faith is void of life; does not exist. However, loosely speaking, the two can be said to mean the same thing, and are often used interchangeably.

Matthew 17:20

20 So Jesus said to them, "Because of your
   unbelief, for assuredly, I say to you,
   if you have faith as a mustard seed,
   you will say to this mountain,
   'Move from here to there,'
   and it will move;
   and nothing will be impossible for you."

To the question by His disciples seeking to know why they could not cast out a demon, Jesus told them it was because of the unbelief in their hearts. He said if they had just a little faith, they would have acted it out. While it looks like belief and faith are used here to mean the same thing, Jesus' use of the word, 'unbelief,' for a state of heart, and 'faith' to depict an action, are still evident, even if just slightly.

Very importantly though, He pointed out that the amount of faith they needed was very little - "as a mustard seed." Also using the same imagery of moving a mountain from one point to the other, in Mk. 11:22-23, and the role of faith in accomplishing this, Jesus admonished His disciples, "Have faith in God" (Vs. 22). The Bible in Basic English (BBE) renders it, "Have God's faith." This is similar to what Greek scholars say is the more appropriate translation of the original Greek version of the verse: "Have the God-kind of faith."

One key element of the God-kind of faith is seeing things as they can and will be, and not as they are presently. Another is to believe with your words as much as you believe with your heart, i.e. for your words to agree with the belief in your heart. Jesus meant that what His disciples needed was not God's size of faith, which is immeasurable, but its kind. It follows, therefore, that when you see like God sees, even if just to a little degree, you will procure great results.

In the journey to destiny, it is very important to see like God sees. You have to train your 'eyes' to look from God's perspective. There's no better prism to view things through than the word of God.

> **There's no better prism to view things through than the word of God.**

SEEING WELL REALLY MATTERS

After Laban had taken away the male goats that were speckled and spotted, all the female goats that were speckled and spotted, every one that had some white in it, and all the brown ones among the lambs (Gen. 30:35), thereby leaving Jacob with no capital to build on since Jacob's portion in the new arrangement was to be the animals that were of the afore-mentioned kinds, Laban separated himself from Jacob by a journey of three days (Verse 36). That way, he made sure that these animals could not stray into the flocks. Laban was now certain that Jacob was condemned to poverty. To 'unweaned' eyes, that certainly looked to be so.

Jacob's game-changing joker lay in his understanding of how powerful what you see can be to what you produce. What you see is also critical to where you go. **What you see is critical to where you go.** The most important asset any driver has is his sight and not his skill with his hands on the steering wheel or with his feet on the pedals. No matter how great his skills are with the latter two, his journey to wherever would not even begin if he is blind. Even with impaired vision, journeying anywhere will be risky for a driver unless with the aid of (prescription) glasses.

Genesis 30:37-39

37 Now Jacob took for himself rods of green poplar and of the almond and chestnut trees, peeled white strips in them, and exposed the white which was in the rods.

38 And the rods which he had peeled, he set before the flocks in the gutters,

> in the watering troughs where the flocks came to drink, so that they should conceive when they came to drink.
>
> 39 So the flocks conceived before the rods, and the flocks brought forth streaked, speckled, and spotted.

Conception was according to sight, and so was what was born. You will always conceive and deliver what you fix your eyes on. Every invention you see today, the electric bulb, the aeroplane, etc. was first a picture in the mind of its inventor. That is to say that the inventor first saw it before he made it. Whereas, Laban just assumed

Every invention was first a picture in the mind of its inventor.

that the animals will produce according to their kind, Jacob knew that he could cause them to produce differently by what he placed before their eyes at the time they conceived.

In life, conception is an on-going affair. You are continually conceiving your future, starting with the next second; the following moment. And you are continually giving birth to the same as the clock continues to tick. It is therefore important that you always have before your 'eyes' what you desire to give birth to. Dr. Oyedepo said, "It's in the future that you picture that you'll feature."

In order not to leave Laban completely without any significant form of increase, Jacob, having proven the efficacy of his formula, then restricted its use to the conception of the stronger livestock. He had the weaker ones conceive without beholding the rods. By so doing, the stronger livestock were Jacob's and the weaker ones Laban's (Vs. 41-42).

THE HEART AND VISION

In biblical terms, the heart is the seat of the intellect, emotions (and affections), and will. It consists of the mind, with which you think, the emotions, with which you feel, and the will, with which you choose. Romans 10:10 says, "For with the heart one believes ...." It is with the heart that you believe, and not with your mind, with which you only think.

Believing is therefore more powerful than thinking since involves the real but unseen world.

Hebrews 11:1 (NIV)

1   Now faith is being sure of what we hope
    for and certain of what we do not see.

On your way to destiny, it is essential to grow your faith. I heard Archbishop Sam Amaga say in 1995, "If you do not grow in faith, you will groan in life." Since faith is seeing the way God sees, the way to do that is to feed your heart with the word of God.

"So then faith comes by hearing, and hearing by the word of God" (Rom. 10:17). 'Hearing' here speaks of intake. Faith comes via the intake of God's word.

The two major gateways to the heart are the eyes and the ears. What your eyes see and focus on and what your ears hear and you give heed to, will definitely impact upon the state of your heart. Jesus said, "Take heed what you hear..." (Mk. 4:24) and, "...take heed how you hear ....." (Lk. 8:18). He wasn't not talking about hearing the audible words but accepting or giving heed to what was said. He said His sheep will not follow a stranger because they do not know his voice (Jn. 10:5).

Sight is a function of the eyes while vision is a function of the heart. I said in Chapter 1, "Vision is foresight with insight, having confidence on (God's) oversight. It is seeing the future as a consequence of your understanding of God's plan and purpose of your life, being confident that God is watching over you as you move in that direction." To say that vision is indispensable in your journey to destiny is to state the obvious.

Proverbs 4:23
23 Keep your heart with all diligence,
    for out of it spring the issues of life.

To keep your heart is to keep your vision, as vision is a function of the heart. Also, destiny and reaching it are major issues of life. The popular poet, Helen Keller (1880-1968), became blind when she was just eighteen months old. Yet, writing in Braille, she became one of the greatest poets that ever lived. When, in old age, she was asked what she thought to be worse than being blind, she said it was having sight without vision.

Physical sight is seeing things as they are. Vision is seeing things as they could be. It does not matter how the circumstances around you look to the physical eyes, yours and those of others. You can see beyond them to where God is taking you.

The understanding of the great power of vision, which he verified even with animals, catapulted Jacob, whom Laban thought was foolish and had been left with nothing, to becoming exceedingly prosperous. He became far richer than Laban.

Genesis 31: 1, 9

1   Now Jacob heard the words of Laban's sons, saying, "Jacob has taken away all that was our father's, and from what was our father's he has acquired all this wealth."

9. So God has taken away the livestock of your father and given them to me.

Wealth does travel or transfer on the wings of vision. What do you see? If you're not seeing anything, you've got to 'stir up' yourself to begin to see something. Begin to see whatever is congruent with God's purpose for you.

Wealth does travel or transfer on the wings of vision.

Like Jacob proved, whatever you see is what you will produce. If that can be true for animals, it is even truer for you. Correspondingly, to see with the eyes of your heart is to believe.

Romans 4:18 (NIV)

18 Against all hope, ABRAHAM in hope
   BELIEVED AND SO BECAME the father
   of many nations, just as it had been said
   to him. "So shall your offspring be."

If Abraham believed and became, as you too believe, you will become. Anything you can believe, you can become. Anything you fix the eyes of your mind/heart steadfastly on, you produce or become, with time.

Proverbs 29:18 (AMP)

18 Where there is no vision
   (no revelation of God and His word),
   the people are unrestrained; ...

Visions are 'restrainers'. What you see determines how you act. If you are not seeing anything, you will behave anyhow. If you see yourself becoming a medical doctor, you will take the relevant subjects seriously. Then you will get into medical school. Vision constrains conduct. What you see going forward is what you will enter into. To prosper financially, for example, you must see prosperity. Then you must proceed to the required lifestyle for financial prosperity, including that of giving – giving your tithes, and engaging in other forms of giving.

> **Visions are 'restrainers'. What you see determines how you act. If you are not seeing anything, you will behave anyhow.**

2 Corinthians 3:18 (AMP)

18 And we all, with unveiled face,
   CONTINUALLY SEEING as in a
   mirror the glory of the Lord,
   ARE PROGRESSIVELY BEING
   TRANSFORMED INTO
   His image from (one degree of)
   glory to (even more) glory,
   which comes from the Lord (who is)

the Spirit.

You must decide to continually behold God's promises with the eyes of your mind, or better still, your heart. Even when prevailing situations seem bent on shifting your focus, endeavour to continually fix your eyes on them. As you do so, you are progressively getting transformed to becoming or producing them.

Vision constrains conduct.

Chapter 4

A PENCHANT FOR HARD WORK

Genesis 31:38-42

38 These twenty years I have been with you;
your ewes and your female goats have not
miscarried their young, and I have not
eaten the rams of your flock.

39 That which was torn by beasts
I did not bring to you;
I bore the loss of it.
You required it from my hand,
whether stolen by day or stolen by night.

40 There I was! In the day the drought
consumed me, and the frost by night,
and my sleep departed from my eyes.

41 Thus I have been in your house twenty
years; I SERVED you fourteen years
for your two daughters, and six years
for your flock, and you have changed
my wages ten times.

> 42 Unless the God of my father,
> the God of Abraham and the Fear of
> Isaac, had been with me, surely now
> you would have sent me away
> empty-handed. God has seen my
> affliction and THE LABOUR OF MY
> HANDS, and rebuked you last night.

One truth that comes out very clearly from this discourse as Jacob tries to justify why he and his family fled from Laban's house, after Laban had pursued and caught up with them, was that Jacob was a very hard worker. As cheated by Jacob as Laban felt, he did not contest this truth. When viewed against the background of Jacob's age for the twenty years be served Laban, his industriousness is even better appreciated. Like we saw in Chapter 2 of this book, Jacob, arguably, served Laban from the age of seventy-seven to the age of ninety-seven.

Going, therefore, by the severity of the work contained in the narrative in view, especially that in Verse 40 ("There I was! In the day the DROUGHT CONSUMED ME, and the FROST by night, and my SLEEP DEPARTED from my eyes."), it is certainly amazing that a man that old could not only cope with such work, but did it well. More so, he seemed to have gone about the work with great enthusiasm. To think that he endured the changing of his wages ten times (Verse 41).

Jacob worked his way to relevance in Laban's house. When he made his intention to leave Laban's house and employment after the birth of Joseph in Gen. 30:25-26, having served for fourteen years, Laban said to him, "Please stay, if I have found favour in your eyes, for I have learned by experience that THE LORD HAS BLESSED ME FOR YOUR SAKE" (Gen. 30:27). The increase in wealth which Laban experienced with Jacob working for him was not only a function of the favour of God upon Jacob; it was also a product of Jacob's hard work.

Work is a multiplier.

With Jacob in his employment, Laban progressed from having little to having much (Gen. 30:30). Work is a multiplier. Jacob then stood on the ground of his diligent service and its apparent results to

Work is a promoter.

negotiate for a change of status from employee to partner, and succeeded. Work is a promoter.

DEFINING WORK

The Complete Christian Dictionary for Home and School defines 'work' as "physical or mental effort or exertion especially with a special purpose." In my book, 'You can be the next Success Story,' I said, "Work is the key to unlocking the treasures God put into you. Until you begin to work, you may never realise how much potential is stored up in you. You may never realise how much you can really do. You may continue to underestimate what can come out of you - what you can do and what you can become."

Jacob's stay and work at Laban's certainly unlocked the treasures God had put in him. When he was still with his parents, he probably did not know that he could work as hard and as intelligently as he did when he came to Laban's place. The demands he had to meet to marry Laban's daughters and his desire later on to provide for his family pushed him far beyond what he may have considered to be his limits. Work has a way of extending what you may have considered to be the limits of your capability.

We also see that Jacob's routine and work hours in Laban's house differed greatly from the ones he had in his father's house. In Gen. 25:29-34, when he bought Esau's birthright, we see that Jacob was already at home cooking a stew by the time Esau returned from work. Again, in Gen.

Work has a way of extending what you may have considered to be the limits of your capability.

27:1-29, when he deceived his father, Isaac, into blessing him, we see that he was also at home, and was available for Rebekah to send to bring the animal that she prepared for him (Jacob) to deceive his father with. On the contrary, in Laban's house, we see that Jacob spent many more hours at work.

Genesis 31:40

40 THERE I WAS! In the day the drought

consumed me, and the frost by night,
and my sleep departed from my eyes.

What work is not:

1) WORK IS NOT A CURSE.

Genesis 2:15 (NIV)
15 The LORD God took the man and put him
in the Garden of Eden TO WORK it and
take care of it.

Work was already in God's programme for man before man sinned. Work was, therefore, not a consequence of sin; was not and is not a curse. Sin only changed the content and conditions of work.

Genesis 3:17-19

17 Then to Adam He said, "Because you have
heeded the voice of your wife,
and have eaten from the tree of which
I commanded you, saying,
'You shall not eat of it':
Cursed is the ground for your sake;
In toil you shall eat of it all the days
of your life.

18 Both thorns and thistles it shall bring
   forth for you, and you shall eat the herb
   of the field.

19 In the sweat of your face you shall eat
   bread till you return to the ground,
   for out of it you were taken;
   For dust you are, And to dust you
   shall return."

Thank God that in Christ, these content and conditions of work have been taken away.

2) WORK IS NOT PUNISHMENT

Some people see work, not as a curse, but as punishment. Of course, the difference between a curse and punishment is that a curse is longer lasting than a punishment. A curse remains until it is broken while a punishment is just for a period of time. Even then, work is not a punishment, as we can see from Gen. 2:15.

3) WORK IS NOT UNAVAILABLE

Jobs may not be available, but work is definitely available. The reasons many people are idle is that they are so intensely focussed on their search for jobs that they have not given any other form of work any thought. Even when no person

Even when no person or organisation seems ready to offer you a job, you can work. Locate the gifts and potentials God has placed in you and put them to work.

or organisation seems ready to offer you a job, you can work. Locate the gifts and potentials God has placed in you and put them to work. As you do so, God will bless your efforts and soon you will be the one offering people jobs.

4)   WORK IS NOT VERY DIFFICULT

Perception is what determines reception. Someone said the reason people miss opportunities to move forward in life is that opportunities are usually dressed in overalls that

What you are seeing as work is simply an opportunity to rise to the next level.

portray them as work. What you are seeing as work is simply an opportunity to rise to the next level.

What work is:

1)   WORK IS A REFLECTION OF THE BLESSING

The blessing is empowerment to prosper and to succeed (Gen. 1:28). The blessing is what births blessings, i.e. blessings are by-products of the blessing. For example, a house is not the blessing; it is just a blessing. The blessing therefore empowers unto wealth.

Work also empowers unto wealth. The blessing and work, thus, belong to the same genre.

Proverbs 10:22
22 The blessing of the LORD makes one rich, and He adds no sorrow with it.

2)   WORK IS A GATEWAY TO BLESSINGS

From (1) above, if work is a reflection of the blessing, work is therefore a channel through which blessings – money, houses, cars, marriage, sound health, etc., come.

3)   WORK IS NOBLE

Work is not something to be ashamed of. It is something to be proud of – no matter the type of work. As long as it is godly, it is honourable.

2 Thessalonians 3:10

10 For even when we were with you,
     we commanded you this:
     If anyone will not work, neither shall
     he eat.

4)   WORK IS FULFILLING

When you work, you are fulfilled. The reason is that you were made to work. And so, when you are idle, you feel empty; you feel like there is something you are lacking.

When you work, you are fulfilled. The reason is that you were made to work.

Ecclesiastes 5: 18-19

18 Here is what I have seen: It is good and
     fittingbfor one to eat and drink, and to
     enjoy the good of all his labour in which
     he toils under the sun all the days of

his life which God gives him; for it
is his heritage.

19 As for every man to whom God has given
riches and wealth, and given him power
to eat of it, to receive his heritage and
rejoice in his labour – this is the gift of God.

THE LAZINESS/IDLENESS – POVERTY CONNECTION

Proverbs 6:9-11 (NIV)

9 How long will you lie there, you sluggard?
When will you get up from your sleep?

10 A little sleep, a little slumber, a little
folding of the hands to rest –

11 and poverty will come on you like a thief
and scarcity like an armed man.

Proverbs 10:4 (NIV)

4 Lazy hands make a man poor, but diligent
hands bring wealth.

Proverbs 14:23 (NIV)

23 All hard work brings a profit, but mere
talk leads only to poverty.

There is a direct correlation between laziness/idleness and poverty. Actually to be poor does not address your financial/material status as much as it addresses your activity status. The Greek word for poor, as used by Jesus, is 'poucos,' and it means 'non-productivity.' That is the true definition of poverty. To be poor means that you are not doing any work. It does not really mean that you do not have anything.

You can, therefore, see that a lazy or idle man is a poor man, and not that he is going to be poor. Also, the man that is productive, that is busy doing something meaningful, is already rich. It's not that he is going to be rich. It is, therefore, correct to say that poverty can be eradicated or cured by meaningful work.

A man who relies on others for his needs and

A man who relies on others for his needs and desires as a result of laziness is a thief.

desires as a result of laziness is also a thief. According to Dr. Myles Munroe, "..., a thief is someone who relies on the productiveness of another to provide for his needs because he is too lazy to meet them himself. If you are able to work and you're not working, you are stealing from those who are working. ... Taking the benefits of work without participating in the effort is theft."

Ephesians 4:28 (NIV)

28 He who has been stealing must steal
    no longer, but must work, doing
    something useful with his own hands, ...

THE POTENCY OF WORK

Nehemiah 2: 17-18

17 Then I said to them, "You see the
    distress that we are in, how Jerusalem
    lies waste and its gates are burned
    with fire. Come and LET US BUILD
    the wall of Jerusalem,

THAT WE MAY NO LONGER
BE A REPROACH."

18 And I told them of the hand of my
God which had been good upon me,
and also of the king's words that he had
spoken to me. So they said,
"Let us rise up and build."
Then THEY SET THEIR HANDS
TO THIS GOOD WORK.

Nehemiah 6:2-3 (NIV)

2   Sanballat and Geshem sent me this
message: "Come, let us meet together
in one of the villages on the plain of Ono."
But they were scheming to harm me;

3   So I sent messengers to them with this
reply: "I AM CARRYING ON A GREAT
PROJECT and cannot go down. Why
should the work stop while I leave it
and go down to you?"

The reason many people are not moving forward
in life is that they loathe work. According to Jim
Michaels, a television journalist in Louisville,
Kentucky, "Too many workers would rather get

home than get ahead." Even when some people manage to get themselves to start working, they are only able to maintain the motivation to do so for a while. As soon as they have the slightest excuse to do so, they stop working.

Consider Nehemiah's response to Sanballat and Geshem: "... I am doing a great work, so that I cannot come down ..." (Neh. 6:3, NKJV).

The perfect will of God for His children is the blessing and not miracles.

Every work that is meaningful; that moves your life forward, is a great work. Every work that is done on the path of God's purpose for you; on your 'purposeway', is a great work. You must resist every attempt to abandon it before completion.

Miracles are introduced by God to make up for lost time/speed, when there has been a season of the absence of the blessing in the life of someone.

In Nigeria, where I live, there is a great apathy towards work. That is the reason many people are looking for jobs, especially government jobs. They do not want to work and, of course, with a lot of the government jobs in my country, you don't really have to work.

Many believers prefer to get ahead on the 'wings' of miracles than on those of work. The truth, however, is that the perfect will of God for His children is the blessing and not miracles (Gal. 3:13-14; Prov. 10:22; Ps. 133:1-3). Miracles are introduced by God to make up for lost time/speed, when there has been a season of the absence of the blessing in the life of someone. And, like I said earlier in this chapter, work is a reflection of the blessing.

When you work your way to wealth, you acquire the maturity to retain and even multiply the wealth.

Work is powerful! Work reveals possibilities! And work qualifies a person for rest. God worked for six days and entered His rest as far as creation was concerned. 'Rest', in this context, does not speak of cessation of work. God is still working (Jn. 5:17). 'Rest' is only indicative of celebration of 'reward' for work accomplished. When you too work sufficiently, you will receive your 'reward'. You will enter your rest.

The wisdom in getting ahead via hard work has also been attested to by research that showed that ninety-eight percent of lottery winners become broke within twenty-four months after they received the money they won. When you work your way to wealth, you acquire the maturity to retain and even multiply the wealth. Hard work is a maturation process for the worker.

Hard work is a maturation process for the worker.

THE PARTNERSHIP BETWEEN WORK AND IDEAS

Exodus 25:40

40 And see to it that you MAKE them according to the PATTERN which was shown you on the mountain.

The great American inventor and businessman, Thomas Edison (1847-1931), made a statement that I find very instructive, especially considering the man that made it. He said, "Genius is one

"Genius is one percent inspiration and ninety-nine percent perspiration."

percent inspiration and ninety-nine percent perspiration." Edison was, by every standard, a genius. He held over one thousand patents for his inventions which included the incandescent electric light bulb, the phonograph and the motion picture camera. He is considered to have been more responsible for creating the modern world than anyone else.

Yet, he considered hard work to have been more responsible for his numerous inventions than the bright ideas his great mind conceived. He thought perspiration to be of greater consequence than inspiration in accomplishing great things. This should increase the value you have for work.

In Exodus 25:40, God was telling Moses to ensure that the building of the tabernacle (and its components) referring to the WORK, was done in line with the pattern, referring to the IDEAS, God had given to Moses. While ideas constitute the 'foundation' for a project or venture, work is the 'superstructure'. As it is with a regular building, the superstructure will usually be 'bigger' than the foundation. This shows us the wisdom in what Thomas Edison said.

Proverbs 16:3

3   Commit your works to the LORD,
      and your thoughts will be established.

It is works, therefore, that establish thoughts (i.e. ideas). Like I also wrote in my book, 'You can be the next Success Story' (Page 129), "It is perspiration that will give expression to your inspiration. It is work - indeed, hard work – that will give form to the gift or talent in you. Until you give the partnership of your perspiration to your inspiration, you will never arrive at your destination."

It is perspiration that will give expression to your inspiration.

Until you give the partnership of your perspiration to your inspiration, you will never arrive at your destination.

Proverbs 12:27

27 The lazy man does not roast what

he took in hunting, but diligence is man's precious possession.

Proverbs 19:24

24 A lazy man buries his hand in the bowl, and will not so much as bring it to his mouth again.

Whatever the quality or quantity of resources available to a lazy man; however great the potentials in him may be, he will still manage to fail. Jacob did have a number of powerful resources, especially spiritual ones, which put him in good stead to succeed. He had God's grace and consistent guidance. He also had his father, Isaac's blessing. However, he needed to be hard working in order to make it to his destiny.

Whatever the leverage you enjoy in life, you must give it the partnership of hard work. The way to your destiny is the way of diligence; the way of hard work.

ABILITY AND SKILL SHOULD UNDERPIN WORK

Exodus 31:1-7

1   Then the LORD spoke to Moses, saying:

2   "See, I have called by name Bezalel
the son of Uri, the son of Hur,
of the tribe of Judah.

3   And I have filled him with the Spirit of
God, in wisdom, in understanding,
in knowledge, and in all manner of
workmanship,

4   to design artistic works, to work in gold,
in silver, in bronze,

5   in cutting jewels for setting,
in carving wood, and to work in all
manner of workmanship.

6   "And I, indeed I, have appointed
with him Aholiab the son of Ahisamach,
of the tribe of Dan; and I have put
wisdom in the hearts of all the gifted
artisans, that they may make all that
I have commanded you:

7   the tabernacle of meeting, the ark

of the Testimony and the mercy seat that is on it, and all the furniture of the tabernacle -

> **To do work that is underpinned by ability and skill is to work wisely.**

To do work that is underpinned by ability and skill is to work wisely. Wisdom is the correct application of knowledge. Wise work usually wins. Wise work usually procures the desired goal(s).

Everybody has one thing that he/she can do pretty well. That is to say that everyone has one ability or the other. There is something you do well, and better than many other people. Skill is simply pruned, polished or developed ability.

Romans 12:6 (NLT)

6 In his grace, God has given us different gifts for doing certain things well...

Just like God required Bezalel, Aholiab and the other gifted artisans to use the abilities He had put in them to build the tabernacle and its various components, God wants you to use the abilities He has blessed you with to build your life and the lives of others. Your abilities and skills give you comparative advantage. When you work in the arena of your gifting, the work is not only normally easier for you to do, but is also usually more rewarding and more fulfilling.

> **When you work in the arena of your gifting, the work is not only easier, but is more rewarding and more fulfilling.**

When Joseph took five of his brothers to see Pharaoh in Genesis 47:2-3, after their arrival in Egypt, Pharaoh asked them, "What is your occupation?" They answered, "Your servants are shepherds, both we and also our fathers." Jacob, their father, had been a shepherd from youth. He had great ability in taking care of livestock as seen from his performance while working for his uncle, Laban.

You can build (the tabernacle of) your life. The wise way to do so is to go the way of your God-given ability. As you exercise your ability, it develops to skill, and facilitates success: "If the axe is dull and its edge unsharpened, more strength is needed but SKILL WILL BRING SUCCESS" (Ecclesiastes 10:10, NIV).

Chapter 5

A LIFESTYLE OF PRAYER

Genesis 32:22-29

22 And he arose that night and took his
two wives, his two female servants,
and his eleven sons, and crossed over the
ford of Jabbok.

23 He took them, sent them over the brook,
and sent over what he had.

24 The Jacob was left alone, and a
Man wrestled with him until the breaking
of day.

25 Now when He saw that He did not prevail
against him, He touched the socket of his
hip; and the socket of Jacob's hip was out
of joint as He wrestled with him.

26 And He said, "Let Me go, for the day
breaks." But he said, "I will not let You go
unless You bless me!"

27 So He said to him, "What is your name?"
He said, "Jacob."

28 And He said, "Your name shall no
   longer be called Jacob, but Israel;
   for you have struggled with
   God and with men, and have prevailed."

29 Then Jacob asked, saying,
   "Tell me Your name, I pray." And
   He said, "Why is it that you ask about My
   name?" and He blessed him there.

Arguably the most defining moment in Jacob's march to destiny, but clearly the most resounding one, relates to prayer. Jacob's encounter with God at Peniel was one of fervent, prevailing prayer. The fact that the encounter lasted the whole night and the manner in which Jacob persisted, refusing to let go until he received the blessing he desired, showed that Jacob was a man of prayer.

Before this encounter, he had also prayed at Mahanaim in Genesis 32:9-12 reminding God that it was He who told him to return to his country, and He (God) will prosper him. He did not forget to acknowledge that God had blessed him abundantly and how unworthy he was of

God's great faithfulness to him thus far. Thinking that Esau, whom he had been told was on the way to meet him, was coming to attack him, he also asked God for protection from him.

Jacob had a lifestyle of prayer. He communed with God regularly. It was therefore fitting that God blessed him in the place of prayer; in the place where he was alone with God.

The critical role of prayer in our Christian walk cannot be over-emphasized. No wonder Paul said we should pray always (1 Thess. 5:17). Life is full of bumpy roads. There is therefore the great need for prayer for one to navigate them successfully.

In the parable of the wicked judge and the widow in Luke 18, Jesus made it clear that God's own elect needed to cry out to God "day and night" (Lk. 18:7). He said that as they did that, God will "avenge them speedily" (Lk. 18:8). That is to say that, as believers pray, God will deliver them from the challenges that abound in life, and make their journey through it smoother.

LOCATING YOUR ALTAR OF INCENSE

Exodus 30:1-2, 6-10

1 "You shall make an altar to burn incense on; you shall make it of acacia wood.

2 "A cubit shall be its length and a cubit its width – it shall be square – and two cubits shall be its height. Its horns shall be of one piece with it."

6 "And you shall put it before the veil that is before the ark of the Testimony, before the mercy seat that is over the Testimony, where I will meet with you.

7 "Aaron shall burn on it sweet incense every morning; when he tends the lamps, he shall burn incense on it.

8 "And when Aaron lights the lamps at twilight, he shall burn incense on it, a perpetual incense before the LORD throughout your generations.

9 "You shall not offer strange incense on it, or a burnt offering, or a grain offering; nor shall you pour a drink on it.

10 "And Aaron shall make atonement

upon its horns once a year with
the blood of the sin offering of
atonement; once a year he shall make
atonement upon it
throughout your generations.
It is most holy to the LORD."

During the journey of the Israelites from Egypt to Canaan, God spoke to Moses that the people should make a sanctuary for Him that would symbolize His presence in their midst (Ex. 25:8). God then gave Moses instructions on how to build the tabernacle (i.e. the sanctuary) and its different parts. The altar of incense was a part of the tabernacle.

The tabernacle, when the Israelites were in the wilderness, and the temple built by Solomon, when they got to Canaan, prefigured the believer, now the dwelling place of God (1 Cor. 3:16; 1 Cor. 6:19). And just like the altar of incense was a very important part of the tabernacle, a believer's prayer life is a very important part of his Christian life. Incense symbolises prayer (Ps. 141:2; Rev. 5:8).

Every believer needs to locate his altar of incense appropriately. 'Locating' here is not about finding out, discovering or seeing where it is. It's about putting it in its proper place; planting it where it should be. Prayer must occupy a place of importance; a place of prominence, in your life; in your daily schedule.

God's instructions to Moses concerning the altar of incense bring out some fundamental truths about prayer:

1)   Prayer is not optional; it is a must (Ex. 30:7-8). The New International Version (NIV) makes this clearer:

Exodus 30:7-8 (NIV)

7   "Aaron MUST burn fragrant incense on the altar every morning ...

8   "He MUST burn incense again when he lights the lamps..."

Aaron, therefore, was not at liberty to decide whether or not to burn incense. It was compulsory for him to do so. Jesus affirmed this truth in Luke 11:2 when He said, "When you pray, ..." He did not say, "If you pray, ..."

2)   It is your responsibility to pray, indeed to develop a prayer life, and not somebody else's (Ex. 30:1, 6-8).

While it okay for others to pray for and with you at times (James 5:14; Mtt. 18:19), the onus primarily rests on you to pray for yourself. You must be your number one prayer vessel.

3)   You should pray regularly and consistently (Ex. 30:7-8).

Aaron was required to burn incense every morning and every evening, making it "a PERPETUAL incense before the LORD..." (Ex. 30:8).

Prayer is usually more effective when it is regular and consistent. Irregular and inconsistent prayer is indicative of insufficient zeal, lack of seriousness, laziness or lack of faith. Heaven does not pay much attention to such prayer (Lk. 11:5-10; Lk. 18:1; 1 Thess. 5:17; Rom. 12: 11-12).

4) In prayer, your vertical connection with God is more important than your horizontal connection with men (Ex. 30:2).

As far as receiving positive answers to your prayers is concerned, what men think and say of you is of no consequence. It is what God thinks of you that counts. The height of the altar of incense (two cubits) was twice its length and width (one cubit each).

As long as God approves of you, the disapproval of you by men holds no water.

As long as God approves of you, the disapproval of you by men holds no water. His dealing with Cornelius and his fellow Gentiles in Acts 10 makes this clear.

God's opinion of Job, as against what his friends thought of him, was what mattered at the end. In Job 42:10, Job got restored after he prayed for his friends. Before then, the friends had labelled Job a sinner in view of the tragedies that befell him.

The great importance of connecting with God is the reason that, even though the altar of incense stood in the Holy Place (Ex. 30:6), the author of Hebrews described it as belonging to the Most Holy Place in Hebrews 9:3-4.

5)   Prayer is a dialogue, not a monologue (Ex. 30:6).

In prayer you don't just talk to God; you talk with God. Your prayer life can only be as potent and productive as it should be when you learn to hear from God as you talk with Him in prayer.

6)   Prayer is the foundational means of securing God's forgiveness (Ex. 30:10).

Under the Old Testament, on the Day of Atonement, the high priest took incense from the alter of incense, along with the blood of the sin offering, into the Most Holy Place, to make atonement for his sins and the sins of the people (Heb. 9:7). But, under the New Testament, with Jesus having shed His blood to atone for our sins (Rom. 5:11; Eph. 1:7; 1 Jn. 2:2), whenever we sin, all we need to do is to pray to God to forgive us (1 Jn. 1:9). Even in the Old Testament, when Israel had sinned, the prophet Hosea told them, "Take words with you, and return to the LORD.

Say to Him, 'Take away all iniquity; receive us graciously, for we will offer the sacrifices of our lips' " (Hosea 14:2).

7)   Prayer must be from a pure heart (Ex. 30:9).

God knows your heart through and through and so you cannot hide anything from Him. Therefore, always come to Him in prayer with a heart void of offence and negative motives (Lev. 10:1; Ps. 66:18).

8)   Giving is not a substitute for prayer or a prayer life (Ex. 30:9).

God longs to have you and Him communicate through prayer and therefore, your giving cannot take the place of prayer. More so, prayer is not only about requesting one thing or the other from God. Actually, it is usually the ungodly that seek to 'bribe' God with their giving and try to avoid talking with Him. God detest this (Prov. 15:8).

As God's dwelling place, you've got to put your 'altar of incense' in its proper position. You have to give prayer the place of prominence it deserves in your life. In this journey to your destiny through the wilderness called life, it is important that the fire on your prayer altar does not go out.

THE PROPER MINDSET IN PRAYER

Luke 11:1-13

1   Now it came to pass, as He was praying
    in a certain place, when He ceased, that
    one of his disciples said to Him, "Lord,
    teach us to pray, as John also taught
    his disciples."

2   So He said to them, "When you pray, say:
    Our Father in heaven,
    Hallowed be Your name.
    Your kingdom come.
    Your will be done on earth
    as it is in heaven.

3   Give us day by day our daily bread.

4   And forgive us our sins, for we also
    forgive everyone who is indebted to us.
    And do not lead us into temptation,
    but deliver us from the evil one."

5   And He said to them,
    "Which of you shall have a friend,

and go to him at midnight and say to him,
'Friend, lend me three loaves;

6 for a friend of mine has come to me on
his journey, and I have nothing to set
before him';

7 and he will answer from within and say,
'Do not trouble me; the door is now shut,
and my children are with me in bed;
I cannot rise and give to you'?

8 I say to you, though he will not rise and
give to him because he is his friend,
yet because of his persistence he will rise
and give him as many as he needs.

9 "So I say to you, ask,
and it will be given to you;
seek, and you will find; knock,
and it will be opened to you.

10 For everyone who asks receives,
and he who seeks finds,
and to him who knocks it will
be opened.

11 If a son asks for bread from any
father among you, will he give him
a stone? Or if he asks for a fish, will he

give him a serpent instead of a fish?

12 Or if he asks for an egg, will he offer
him a scorpion?

13 If you then, being evil, know how to
give good gifts to your children,
how much more will your
heavenly Father give the Holy Spirit to
those who ask Him!"

We see also from Verse 5 to 8 of Luke 11 that prayer is a dialogue and not a monologue, like I said earlier. The Lord's Prayer in Verse 2 to 4 and the parable in Verse 5 to 8 do not only teach the right principles/pattern of prayer but also the proper mindset to pray effectively. The better your mindset is when you pray, the more potent your prayer will be.

(1)   As you pray, always remember that God is
        your Father, i.e. always pray with a family
        mindset; a freedom mindset;
        a friendship mindset (Lk. 11:2).

You are not a slave/servant. You are not in bondage. You have unhindered/unrestricted access to God, and He has to you also. A child of God can only be called a servant of God in the sense of being a minister of the gospel, i.e. a worker in God's vineyard.

The elder brother of the prodigal son had to be told by his father of his privileged position in his father's house (Lk. 15:31). The reason most believers cannot pray effectively is because they see themselves as cut off from God by one thing or the other – a curse, background, barrier, the past, etc. That is the devil's trick and lie to keep them from getting what is theirs.

(2)   As you pray, let the good of
        God's kingdom occupy a pole position
        in your heart (Lk. 11:2).

When you make God's business your business, God will make your business His business.

When you make God's business your business, God will make your business His business.

Praying that God's kingdom comes is not only asking for the advent of the messianic kingdom age, but also the expansion of His kingdom now – for souls to be saved/won into His kingdom/family.

(3)   As you pray, be concerned about
      others (Lk.11:3).

Every child of God is a priest
(1 Pet. 2:9; Rev. 1:6) and should
therefore represent God's people
before God. Where there is
heartfelt intercession, there will
be restoration (Joel 2:17-20, 25).

Where there is heartfelt intercession, there will be restoration.

(4)   As you pray, delight in righteousness
      (Lk. 11:4).

You cannot be communicating with a holy God and at the same time be romancing sin in (a corner of) your heart. Like we saw earlier with regards to the altar of incense, prayer must be from a pure heart (Ex. 30:9). You know it is possible to be praying to God and trusting Him for one blessing or the other and at the same time be hungry for or even planning unrighteousness. That is a most unwholesome mindset in prayer.

(5)   As you pray, look forward to answers
      from God (Lk. 11:9-10).

God answers every earnest prayer. He will either

say, "Yes," "No," or "Not yet." You must therefore pray with faith in your heart. A heart with faith is an indication of maturity and is more likely to get God to give a "Yes" answer.

6)   As you pray, get ready for
      the Holy Spirit (Lk. 11:13; Mtt. 7:11).

Matthew 7:11, which is the corresponding Scripture to Luke 11:13 talks about God giving "good gifts" to those who ask Him. With Luke 11:13 saying God will give the Holy Spirit to those who ask Him, it is evident that the good gifts in Matthew 7:11mean spiritual gifts. The Holy Spirit is the greatest of God's gifts. God giving the Holy Spirit means God baptizing us with His Spirit and also availing us of the work of the Spirit.

The surest answer you can expect from your prayer is the work of the Holy Spirit. Of course, when the Holy Spirit is at work, you can be sure of enablement, direction, boldness, insight and every other

> **The surest answer you can expect from your prayer is the work of the Holy Spirit.**

ingredient you need for a victorious life. All that you actually need is the work of the Holy Spirit. Prayer puts the Holy Spirit to work in you.

With the Spirit of God at work in you, you are made. With the Spirit of God at work in you, all your heart's desires will fall into place - eventually. With the Spirit of God at

All that you actually need is the work of the Holy Spirit.

work in you, you will reach your destiny. As you pray, let your mindset be one of preparedness for the Holy Spirit.

From what we see of Jacob at Mahanaim and especially at Peniel (both in Genesis 32), he was a man with a great prayer life. He knew how to be earnest and fervent in the place of prayer.

James 5:16-17

16 ... The effective, fervent prayer of a
   righteous man avails much.

17 Elijah was a man with a nature as ours,
   and he prayed earnestly that it would
   not rain; and it did not rain on the land
   for three years and six months.

Romans 12:11

11 not lagging in diligence, fervent in spirit,
   serving the Lord;

Jacob held unto God in prayer even with a
dislocated thigh, that is
to say, at great cost. The
thigh being the strongest
part of the body, to refuse
to let God go even when
it was out of joint tells us how fervently and
persistently Jacob prayed. That in turn showed
how critical to his destiny he saw prayer to be.

> **Prayer puts the Holy
> Spirit to work in
> you.**

Isaiah 62:1, 6-7

1 For Zion's sake I will not hold My peace,
   and for Jerusalem's sake I will not rest,
   until her righteousness goes forth as
   brightness, and her salvation as a lamp
   that burns.

6 I have set watchmen on your walls,
   O Jerusalem; they shall never hold
   their peace day or night. You who make
   mention of the LORD, do not keep silent.

7 And give Him no rest till He establishes

and till He makes Jerusalem a praise in the earth.

Like Jacob, no matter the cost, you must keep your prayer altar aglow. Do not let go of God until you reach your destiny.

Chapter 6

THE MAXIMIZATION OF OPPORTUNITIES

Genesis 32: 22-28

22 And he arose that night and took his
two ies, his two female servants,
and his eleven sons, and crossed over
the ford of Jabbok.

23 He took them, sent them over the brook,
and nt over what he had.

24 The Jacob was left alone, and a Man
wrestled with him until the
breaking of day.

25 Now when He saw that He did not prevail
agaist him, He touched the socket of his
hip; and the socket of Jacob's hip was out
of joint as He wrestled with him.

26 And He said, "Let Me go, for the day
breaks." But he said, "I will not let You go
unless You bless me!"

27 So He said to him, "What is your name?"
He said, "Jacob."

> 28 And He said, "Your name shall no longer
> be called Jacob, but Israel; for you have
> struggled with God and with men,
> and have prevailed."

Success in life is determined by how effectively we use time. You are a sum total of what you spend your time on. How effectively you used your time in the past is

You are a sum total of what you spend your time on.

responsible for who and what you are today, and how you spend your time today will determine who and what you will be tomorrow.

Time is one of the five types of resources that God has given you which you must appreciate and invest wisely if you are to become a success story in life; if you are to become who and what made you to be. The others are spiritual resources, physical resources, material resources, and resources of the soul. The wise and effective use of these resources will ensure that you make it to your destiny.

Time is a temporary interruption in eternity.

Time was God's first creation, that is, on the first day (Gen. 1:3-5). The reason there could be a first day (Vs. 5) was that God, who lived (and still lives)

Time is a temporary interruption in eternity.

outside of time; in an eternal now, had created time with the creation of light (which He called Day) and darkness (which He called Night).

Time is a resource that God has given to every individual equally. It can neither be bought nor sold. You can only use it. If you do not use it, you will lose it.

Jacob was a wise and effective user of time. All through his life, we see in him a determination to make every moment count. Immediately he realised that God was with him at Bethel (Gen. 28:16-17), he seized the opportunity and made a vow to God (Gen. 28:20-22), like we saw in Chapter Two of this book.

Genesis 28:16-17

16 Then Jacob awoke from his sleep and said, "Surely the LORD is in this place, and I did not know it."

17 And he was afraid and said,
   "How awesome is this place!
   This is none other than the house of God,
   and this is the gate of heaven."

Genesis 28:20-22

20 Then Jacob made a vow, saying,
   "If God will be with me, and keep me in
   this way that I am going, and give me
   bread to eat and clothing to put on,

21 "so that I come back to my father's house
   in peace, then the LORD shall be my God.

22 "And this stone which I have set as a
   pillar shall be God's house, and of all that
   You give me I will surely give a
   tenth to You."

Considering the fact that the proofs of God's presence there at Bethel, angels ascending and descending a ladder that was set up on the earth with its top reaching to heaven, and God talking to him, were in a dream, you could very well say that Jacob made the most of that opportunity. When he, therefore, encountered God in Peniel while awake in Gen. 32:22-28, it was understandable that he again maximised the moment, and the night became a life-transforming one for him.

Ephesians 5:15-16 (NIV)

15 Be very careful, then, how you live –
not as unwise but as wise,

16 making the most of every opportunity,
because the days are evil.

The way to live wisely is to make the most of every opportunity. To do otherwise, and to keep letting opportunities slip by, is to live foolishly. And the foolish do not reach their city; they do not reach their destiny. Actually, they either do not know or do not recognise the way to it.

Ecclesiastes 10:15

15 The labour of fools wearies them, for they
do not even know the way to go to the city!

It takes wisdom to get to your destiny. And one sure way to be wise is to make the most of opportunities that come your way. The truth is that opportunities come your way every day. Opportunities are not limited to circumstances from which you can make financial and/or material profit.

Every day presents you with several opportunities to pray; to study God's word; to learn one good thing or the other; to do one form of good or the other to someone. "Therefore, as we have opportunity, let us do good ..." (Gal. 6:10). You may not see any profit resulting from seizing these opportunities or the foreseeable derivables from them many not look attractive or worth your while. With time however, as you continue to make the most of these opportunities, you will be glad you did.

Psalm 90:12 (KJV)

> 12 So teach us to number our days, that we may apply our hearts unto wisdom.

Time is the currency of life. Currency is the medium of exchange used in an economy to purchase goods and services. In the same way money is the currency of a nation's economy, time is the currency of life. Therefore, just like money is used to buy things, you could

Time is the currency of life. Like money is used to buy things, time is used to buy life.

say that time is used to buy life. And just like every nation's currency has units, time too has units: millennia, centuries, decades, years, months, weeks, days, hours, minutes, and seconds.

The more serious you are about management of time or maximizing the moment, the smaller the unit of time you will be concerned about. People that really value their time and want to manage same as efficiently as possible try to make sure that they spend every minute of their days profitably. It was the dire need to maximise the moment that made the Psalmist to pray in Ps. 90:12 that God should teach us to number our days (and not our years) so that we could live wisely. By living wisely, he meant maximising our days.

The more serious you are about management of time or maximizing the moment, the smaller the unit of time you will be concerned about.

THE BEAUTY OF NOW

Ecclesiastes 9:11

11 I returned and saw under the sun that -

> The race is not to the swift, nor the
> battle to the strong, nor bread to
> the wise, nor riches to men of
> understanding, nor favour to men of skill;
> but time and chance happen to them all.

According to Bishop T.D Jakes, "Life is a hyphen locked between two dates. It is the gap between two appointments." This is to say, for example, that when writing about a man that is no more, we say, Mr. Johnbull Gorimapa (1920-2000). The hyphen between those two dates represents the life of Mr. Gorimapa. It is critical to maximise the time between when you came into this world and when you will exit it. You must endeavour to maximise each moment.

It is critical to maximise the time between when you came into this world and when you will exit it.

The now is beautiful. It's the phase of your time that you are in the greatest position to do something about - now. It's the only aspect of your time that you have some kind of a direct hold on.

The past is gone; the future is yet to come. But the now is here. Your today is here. Of course, the only way you can influence your future is by what you do now.

To have foresight is great. To be visionary is wonderful. However, like I stated in Chapter One, "Foresight is the ability to see a sufficient part of tomorrow (i.e. the future) in order to act appropriately today (i.e. the present)." While looking forward to tomorrow therefore, you must celebrate today, and maximise it.

> **The now is beautiful. It's the phase of your time that you are in the greatest position to do something about - now.**

What the author of Ecclesiastes, probably King Solomon, stated in Ecc. 9:11, were truths that are difficult to contest. The 'races' of life are not necessarily won by the fastest, nor the battles by the strongest; nor food always available to the wise. He also said that skilful people are not necessarily wealthy, and the educated are not always success stories. He concluded that "time and chance" determined how people fared in life.

The word, 'chance', speaks of 'opportunity.' Success can result when people make use of the 'collision' between right time and opportunity. While time is a constant, right time is not. Opportunity is also not a constant. When opportunity 'shows up' therefore at the right time, the appropriate use of it at that time can produce success.

However, Ecclesiastes 9:11, above every other thing, alludes to the sovereignty of God in all matters of life.That was why I said that the appropriate use of the 'collision' or put another way, coincidence, of right time and opportunity CAN produce success. With God's approval or backing, it WILL produce success.

> **Success can result when people make use of the 'collision' between right time and opportunity.**

No wonder Paul said, "I planted, Apollos watered, but God gave the increase" (1 Cor. 3:6). No matter how skilfully the planting and watering were done, it takes God's input for increase to result. The increase therefore, is a testament to

God's sovereignty.

Another good substitute for the word, 'chance', in Ecclesiastes 9:11 is 'circumstance'. The New Living Translation (NLT) renders the last part of the verse this way: "It is all decided by chance, by being in the right place at the right time." Even when you are the right person, therefore, possessing the right skill/ability, you have to be in the right place, and at the right time, for you to accomplish your desired goal.

No matter how skilfully the planting and watering were done, it takes God's input for increase to result.

This is to say that there are certain elements of circumstance that have to be in place for even someone with the necessary skill to achieve success.

Judges 11:9-11

9   So Jephthah said to the elders of Gilead, "If you take me back home to fight against the people of Ammon, and the LORD delivers them to me, shall I be your head?"

10 And the elders of Gilead said to Jephthah.
   "The LORD will be a witness between us,
   if we do not do according to your words."

11 Then Jephthah went with the elders of
   Gilead, and the people made him head
   and commander over them; and Jephthah
   spoke all his words before the LORD
   in Mizpah.

Jephthah was a man who knew how to make the most of opportunities. After his step-brothers had driven him out from his father's house (Judg.11:2), what the elders of Gilead offered Jephthah when Ammon made war with Israel and the need for Jephthah arose, was commandership of their army in the war against Ammon (Judg. 11:6). Jephthah wanted more. He demanded to be both commander and head. Of course, the headship transcended the period of the war.

Philippians 3:13-14

13 Brethren, I do not count myself to
   have apprehended; but one thing I do,
   forgetting those things which are behind

and reaching forward to those
things which are ahead,

14 I press towards the goal for the prize
of the upward call of God in Christ Jesus.

It's wise to 'leave' the past. It's profitable to look forward with hope to the future. However, for you to get to the good located in the future, you must 'live' the present. The most practical way (to move) forward is to press (presently) towards it.

The way to maximise life is to maximise opportunities. To maximise opportunities is to manage time effectively.

And so, though "time and chance" happen to all men; though God has the final say in whether or not men achieve success, it is important to maximise time. It is critical to do what you can when opportunities come at the right time. It is rewarding to do the needful when you are at the right place at the right time. You must maximise opportunities.

The way to maximise life is to maximise

opportunities. To maximise opportunities is to manage time effectively. You must never get tired of doing so because it's never too late to receive a turn-around. It's never too late to receive a new name. By the time God gave Jacob a new name, he was ninety-seven years old, and he already had two wives, two maidservants and eleven children (Gen. 32:22).

> **it's never too late to receive a turn-around. It's never too late to receive a new name.**

THE ATTITUDE OF HUMILITY

Genesis 33: 1-3, 10-11

1   Now Jacob lifted his eyes and looked,
and there, Esau was coming, and
with him were four hundred men.
So he divided the children among Leah,
Rachel, and the two maidservants.

2   And he put the maidservants and their
children in front, Leah and her children
behind, and Rachel and Joseph last.

3   Then he crossed over before them and
BOWED HIMSELF TO THE GROUND
SEVEN TIMES, until he came near to
his brother.

10 And Jacob said, "No, please,
if I have now found favour in your
sight, then receive my present from
my hand, inasmuch as I HAVE SEEN
YOUR FACE AS THOUGH I HAD SEEN
THE FACE OF GOD, and you were
pleased with me.

11 "Please, take my blessing that is brought to you because God has dealt graciously with me, and because I have enough. So he urged him, and he took it.

Prelude to Jacob's encounter with God at Peniel, in Genesis 32, he had sent messengers to his brother, Esau, from Mahanaim, in a bid to douse the anger he thought Esau felt towards him; "... I have been staying with Laban and have remained there till now ... Now I am sending this message to my Lord, THAT I MAY FIND FAVOUR IN YOUR EYES" (Gen. 32:4-5, NIV). When the messengers returned to tell Jacob that Esau was on the way to meet him, and that he had four hundred men with him, fear gripped Jacob.

The meeting proper of the two brothers did not take place until after Jacob had had the encounter with the Lord at Peniel, and God had given him a new name. As it turned out, Jacob's fear that Esau was coming to attack him turned out to be unnecessary. God had also blessed Esau very much (Gen. 33:9) and he no longer bore any grudge against Jacob.

Jacob's actions and words when he met Esau paint a picture of humility. He "bowed himself to the ground seven times" (Gen. 33:3), a symbol of total submission and respect for his big brother. Jacob told Esau that seeing Esau's face was like seeing God's face.

While it could be argued that those actions and words were produced by the fear in Jacob, it must be remembered that Jacob, at this time, did not only have the birthright and the father's blessing but also God's assurance of His (God's) presence, protection and preservation (Gen. 28:15; Gen. 31:3). It makes sense, therefore, to say that what Jacob did and said were borne of genuine humility.

In Genesis 33:11, we also see Jacob acknowledging that the blessing he had was from God and not his struggles, first with Esau, and then with Laban. He said, "Please, take my blessing that is brought to you because God has dealt graciously with me, ... (Gen. 33:11). The Hebrew word rendered "present" in Genesis 33:10 but "blessing" in Genesis 33:11 is the same that is used for "blessing" in Genesis 27:35.

In a manner of speaking, therefore, Jacob, in his determination to reconcile with his brother, gave Esau back the "blessing" he had stolen from him. He took out of the bountiful blessing God had given him to 'return' the stolen one to Esau.

1 Peter 5:5-6 (NIV)

5 Young men, in the same way be
submissive to those who are older.
All of you, clothe yourselves with humility
toward one another, because,
"God opposes the proud but gives
grace to the humble."

6 Humble yourselves, therefore, under
God's mighty hand, that he may lift you
up in due time.

Grace, in the context of Verse 5, means enabling power. God gives power to the humble that enables him/her to move forward. On the contrary, He opposes the advancement of the proud.

Luke 7: 7-8

7 Therefore I did not even think myself
worthy to come to You. But say the word,

and my servant will be healed.

8   For I also AM A MAN PLACED UNDER
AUTHORITY, having soldiers under me.
And I say to one, 'Go,' and he goes;
and to another, 'Come,' and he comes;
and to my servant, 'Do this,' and he does it.

By the time the friends that the centurion that spoke the words in Luke 7:7-8 returned to the centurion's house, they "found the servant well who had been sick" (Verse 10). The exercise of authority is powered, not by what you are set or placed over, but by what you are set under. For you to efficiently and successfully exercise authority, you must be properly set under a higher authority. It's what I call 'the set under advantage.'

> **It takes humility to accept to be under. It takes being under to exercise authority.**

It takes humility to accept to be under. It takes being under to exercise authority. And moving forward in life is easier when you are a man/woman of authority.

Kingdom authority is delegated authority. That

is to say that it is authority that is passed down from a higher or superior authority, in the case of kingdom authority, the ultimate King, God. For you to exercise kingdom authority efficiently and successfully, you must be set under God.

My definition of authority is derived from Genesis 2:19: "Whatever name Adam called each living creature, that was its name." Authority, to me, is giving a situation or thing a name and that becoming its name. Authority is the right to or position from which you give a situation or thing a name and it becomes its name. When you walk in authority, you call into being the desires of your heart.

> **Authority is giving a situation or thing a name and that becoming its name.**

Adam and Eve, before the fall, were persons of authority. However, when they moved away from their position, which was under God, by disobeying Him, they lost the wherewithal to exercise authority. They were banished from the Garden of Eden, the place of pursuit of purpose; the place of all-round prosperity and abundance;

the place of fulfilment of destiny.

A lot of people are more interested in being set over structures than being set under them. In fact, many people do not want to be set under anything. They just want to be set over as many things as possible. Many believers do not want to be subject to God, not to talk about any man, but they want things and situations to be subject to them.

They want to live in disobedience to God while at the same enjoy authority over as many things as possible. And because it just cannot work that way, a number of believers have completely gone astray. That is the reason for the patronage of the devil for his kind of power by some. Of course, it still translates to placing themselves under, only in this case, under the devil.

To be set under God is to walk orderly.

To be set under God is to walk orderly. It is to live a life of consistent obedience to God. It is to align your life with God's word. Only the truly humble can do so. When you do, in due season, God will lift you up; He will promote you.

The path of humility is the path of obedience. And the path of obedience is the highway to destiny. Jacob's father, Isaac, was perhaps richer than Laban, Jacob's maternal uncle. This was even more so at the time Jacob started to work for Laban, which service made Laban far richer than he previously was. Despite his father's status however, Jacob humbled himself and served Laban.

> **The path of humility is the path of obedience. And the path of obedience is the highway to destiny.**

IT TAKES HUMILITY TO SERVE CREDITABLY

Matthew 23:11-12

> 11 But he who is greatest among you shall be your servant.
>
> 12 And whoever exalts himself will be humbled, and he who humbles himself will be exalted.

When there was a dispute amongst Jesus' disciples (in Luke 9:46) as to which of them would be the greatest, Jesus communicated to them the same lesson in Matthew 23:11-12. He told them, "... For he who is least among you all will be great." The way to greatness is humility.

According to C. S. Lewis, "True humility is not thinking less of yourself; it is thinking of yourself less." That is to say that true humility is not low self-esteem, but selflessness. It is being able to put others or their interests before you or your interests.

"True humility is not thinking less of yourself; it is thinking of yourself less."

It takes servant-heartedness to do so.

For the first fourteen (out of the twenty) years that Jacob was with Laban, his major concern was the prosperity of Laban. He served diligently and so fruitfully that Laban prospered abundantly.

True humility is not low self-esteem, but selflessness.

Genesis 30:30

5   For what you had before I came was little, and it has increased to a great amount; the LORD has blessed you since my coming. And now, when shall I also provide for my own house?

For those fourteen years, therefore, Jacob placed Laban's interest before his (Jacob's) own. It wasn't until the end of fourteen years that he decided to also pay significant attention towards providing for himself and his family. And when he made his intention to do that known to Laban, Laban was unable to oppose it, seeing that Jacob had paid his dues.

Luke 16:12

> 12 And if you have not been faithful in what is another man's, who will give you what is your own?

When you have been humble enough to be faithful in what is somebody else's, in due course, God will bless you with your own.

THE MIND OF CHRIST IS THE MAKER OF MEN

Philippians 2:5-11

> 5 Let this mind be in you which was also in Christ Jesus,
>
> 6 who, being in the form of God, did not consider it robbery to be equal with God,

7 but made Himself of no reputation,
  taking the form of a bondservant,
  and coming in the likeness of men.

8 And being found in appearance as a man,
  He humbled Himself and became obedient
  to the point of death, even the death on
  the cross.

9 Therefore God also has highly exalted Him
  and given Him the name which is
  above every name,

10 that at the name of Jesus every knee
  should bow, of those in heaven, and
  of those on earth, and of those under
  the earth,

11 and that every tongue should confess that
  Jesus Christ is Lord, to the
  glory of God the Father.

As with every virtue, Christ is our perfect example of humility. Though God, He agreed to become man and was born in a manger, an open box from which animals feed. He 'descended' further to dying in a shameful way on

Christ is our perfect example of humility.

a cross - the kind of death meant for criminals. All of these He did for the salvation of man.

Such unprecedented humility earned Him His Father's exaltation. God the Father, therefore, gave His Son the name which is above every other name. Humility is a promoter.

Humility is a promoter.

The New International Version renders Philippians 2:5 as, "Your attitude should be the same as that of Christ Jesus." Your attitude will always determine your altitude. When your attitude is that of humility, you are certainly on your way to exaltation. Like I pointed out earlier, Jacob's father, Isaac, was perhaps richer than Laban. Yet, Jacob was humble enough to serve Laban.

1 Samuel 25: 23-24, 27

23 Now when Abigail saw David,
    she dismounted quickly from the donkey,
    fell on her face before David,
    and bowed down to the ground.

24 So she fell at his feet and said:

> "On me, my Lord, on me let this iniquity
> be! And please let your maidservant speak
> in your ears, and hear the words of
> your maidservant."
>
> 27 "And now this present which your
> maidservant has brought to my lord, let it
> be given to the young men who follow
> my lord."

What amazing manifestation of humility in both action and speech! At this time David was in the Wilderness of Paran, on the run from King Saul, who was bent on killing him. Abigail, on the other hand, was the wife of a very rich man by name, Nabal (1 Sam. 25:2-3). Clearly, therefore, David was poorer than Nabal (and, by extension, Abigail). In spite of this, when Abigail heard that her husband had rebuffed the men that David had sent to him to request food, she took immediate steps to assuage the hurt she knew David was feeling.

She went about this with utmost humility. Not only did she bow to the ground before David and fall at his feet before apologising for her husband's misbehaviour, but she further massaged David's ego by asking that what she brought be given to David's followers. Of course, she knew that David too needed the food, and would also partake in the eating.

> **It does not matter where you are in life, high or low. With humility, you are certain to go higher.**

Her humility brought her promotion. When her husband died about ten days later, David sent and proposed to her, to marry her (1 Sam. 25:38-39). She agreed (Vs. 41). When David became king, she became one of his queens.

It does not matter where you are in life, high or low. With humility, you are certain to go higher.

THE HUMBLE WILL HAVE NO PROBLEM WITH BEGINNING SMALL

Job 8:7 (NIV)

7   Your beginning will seem humble,
      so prosperous will your future be.

Zechariah 4:10

10 For who has despised the day of
small things? ...

God wants you to start the journey to that desire of your heart today. Whatever your dream in life may be; however big your vision is, what you have today, where you are right now, is good enough to START with. The money you have; the education you have acquired; the skill you have developed; the beauty you are blessed with, etc., is sufficient to start your journey with.

The tendency a lot of the time is to see yourself as not having enough capital to start any business; not having enough of that needed ingredient to embark on that venture. That is usually the trick of

> **Whatever your dream in life may be, what you have today, where you are right now, is good enough to START with.**

the enemy (i.e. the devil and your flesh) to keep you from beginning. And, of course, what you don't even begin, you cannot ever hope to finish; to actualize.

Gideon thought of himself to be the least even amongst the weakest (Judges 6:15). But God said to him, "Go in this might of yours ... Have I not sent you?" (Judges 6:14). Once you have God's approval concerning any venture, you can start with what you have. You can start where you are. All you need is to be humble, but bold.

At a time Abraham had not as much as annexed one inch of the promised land, God said to him, "Lift your eyes now and look FROM WHERE YOU ARE - northward, southward, eastward, and westward; for all the land which you see I give to you and your descendants forever" (Gen. 13:14-15). The only business that is done from the top to the bottom is grave-digging. And the intention in this case is to keep something from public view forever. But if you desire to see your dream in the domain of public display; if you want your dream to mount the world stage, then you must start from the bottom upwards.

If you want your dream to mount the world stage, then you must start from the bottom upwards.

If you are truly humble, you'll have no qualms at all with starting small. Jacob started small in Laban's house, earning wages. In due course, God promoted him. As you start small, God will also promote you. Your future will be prosperous!

Chapter 8

THE RICHES OF GOD'S GRACE

Genesis 25:21-23

21 Now Isaac pleaded with the LORD for
his wife, because she was barren;
and the LORD granted his plea, and
Rebekah his wife conceived.

22 But the children struggled together within
her; and she said, "If all is well, why am
I like this?" So she went to inquire of the
LORD.

23 And the LORD said to her:
"Two nations are in your womb,
two peoples shall be separated from your
body; one people shall be stronger than
the other, and the older shall serve
the younger."

When the disclosure by God to Rebekah in
Genesis 25:23 is taken into consideration, it
becomes very clear that Jacob was, more than
any other thing, a beneficiary of God's grace.

What God said makes it evident that at the very foundation of Jacob's journey to destiny was his election by God. However, like I wrote in the 'Introduction'. Jacob still needed to align with God's will to make his calling and election sure (2 Pet 1:10). He did that through the qualities we have discussed in the previous seven chapters of this book.

Grace has so many meanings. The ones we see in the Bible are:

(1) the unmerited favour of God
     "For it is by grace you have been saved, ..." (Eph. 2:8, NIV); "and are justified freely by his grace through the redemption that came by Christ Jesus" (Rom. 3:24, NIV);

(2) the application of Christ's righteousness to the sinner – "....
     But where sin increased, grace
     increased all the more, so that, just
     as sin reigned in death, so also
     grace might reign through
     righteousness ..." (Rom. 5:20-21, NIV);

(3)   eternal life; final salvation – "…; set your hope fully on the grace to be given you when Jesus Christ is revealed" (1 Pet. 1:13, NIV);

(4)   virtues proceeding from divine influence, such as faith, meekness, humility, patience, generosity – "…. – see that you also excel in this grace of giving" (2 Cor. 8:7, NIV);

(5)   spiritual power – "And God is able to make all grace abound to you …," (2 Cor. 9:8);

(6)   gratitude – "…., singing with grace in your hearts to the Lord" (Col. 3:16);

(7)   privilege – "…, this grace was given, that I should preach among the Gentiles the unsearchable riches of Christ," (Eph. 3:8); and

(8)   kindness to say and do what is right – "Let your conversation be always full of grace, …" (Col. 4:6, NIV).

The definition in Number 1, 'unmerited favour', is the one of greatest relationship to the subject of our discussion. Like I also said in the 'Introduction', God's election of Jacob even before his birth showcases the fact "that God's people are not products of natural or worldly development, but of His sovereign predetermination and intervention in the affairs of men." And so, though we see Jacob struggle to make it in life; though we see him successfully become the custodian of the Abrahamic covenant, the major anchor of that 'accomplishment' was not his efforts but God's pre-election of him.

God is grace Personified.

Grace and mercy are often used interchangeably in the Bible. That is because both are two sides of the same coin. Grace is God giving you the good you do not deserve, while mercy is God withholding from you the bad that you deserve.

God is grace Personified. Therefore, grace has always been. Paul said God "saved us and called us with a holy calling, not according to our works, but according to HIS OWN purpose and GRACE which was GIVEN TO US in Christ Jesus

BEFORE TIME BEGAN" (2 Tim. 1:9). Though the sacrificial death of Christ ushered us into the dispensation of grace, so-called, that was not the inception of grace. Adam and Eve did not ask to be created. Their creation, therefore, was an act of grace by God.

With the dispensation of grace, however, man now enjoys grace much more than he has ever done, since man's fall. Because of the substitutional death of Jesus died on the cross, God's dealings with man are now majorly on the basis of grace. That's why grace is said to be God's Riches At Christ's Expense.

Romans 9:11-16

11 (for the children not yet being born, nor having done any good or evil, that the purpose of God according to election might stand, not of works but of Him who calls),

12 it was said to her, "The older shall serve the younger."

13 As it is written, "Jacob I have loved, but Esau I have hated."

14 What shall we say then? Is there unrighteousness with God? Certainly not!

15 For He says to Moses, "I will have mercy on whomever I will have mercy, and I will have compassion on whomever I will have compassion."

16 So then it is not of him who wills, nor of him who runs, but of God who shows mercy.

The Bible does not say if Rebekah discussed what God told her about the children in her womb (in Genesis 25:23; referred to by Paul in Romans 9:12) with anybody. We don't know if she told her husband, Isaac, or the 'chosen' son, Jacob, anything about it. The fact that the Bible doesn't say she did, however, suggests that she did not.

What we see, even right from their delivery, with Jacob holding on to Esau's heels as he (Jacob) came out, were intense efforts by Jacob to rule over Esau. If only he had known that God had already willed that he be the more blessed than his brother. Had he known that God had already preferred him; selected him ahead of Esau, he probably would have gone about actualizing his destiny in a different way.

God's election predates creation. If you are a child of God, know it that God elected you before He created the world (and you). Purpose is older than product. A manufacturer's purpose for a product was already in his mind before he went on to produce it.

> **God's election predates creation. God elected you before He created the world (and you).**

Ephesians 1:4-5 (NIV)

4   For he chose us in him before the creation of the world to be holy and blameless in his sight. In love

5   he predestined us to be adopted as his sons through Jesus Christ, in accordance with his pleasure and will –

Even before God made His election, He foreknew creation and how chaotic it would be. He foreknew the challenges you would face in order to fulfil His purpose for you. He foreknew the bumpy road you would travel on the journey to your destiny. And yet He elected you. It follows, therefore,

Purpose is older than product. A manufacturer's purpose for a product was already in his mind before he went on to produce it.

that the challenges; the bumpy road, cannot stop you from reaching your destiny.

Jacob reached his destiny. You too will reach yours!

QUALIFIED BY GRACE

Acts 10:44-48

44 While Peter was still speaking these words, the Holy Spirit fell upon all those who heard the word.

45 And those of the circumcision who believed were astonished, as many as came with Peter, because the gift of the Holy Spirit had been poured out on the Gentiles also.

46 For they heard them speak with tongues and magnify God. Then Peter answered,

47 "Can anyone forbid water, that these should not be baptized who have received

> the Holy Spirit just as we have?"
>
> 48 And he commanded them to be baptized in the name of the Lord. Then they asked him to stay a few days.

In Acts Chapter 9, Dorcas, a disciple whose life had been a blessing to many, died, and the other disciples in Joppa, where she lived, sent for Peter, who was in Lydda at that time. Peter went over to Joppa, prayed for the dead Dorcas and she was raised back to life (Acts 9:40). Peter then remained in Joppa for some time in the house of a tanner named Simon.

In Simon's house, Peter had a vision in which he was hungry but rejected the animals that heaven offered to him to "kill and eat" (Acts 10:13), as Peter called them unclean. After the vision through which God taught him not to regard any man God had cleansed as unclean or impure, Peter did not hesitate to go over to the house of Cornelius (a Gentile) at Caesarea when Cornelius sent for him, in obedience to God's instruction. As Peter was still speaking to the gathering of Gentiles in Cornelius' house, the Holy Ghost fell on all those who heard the message.

This incident further convinced Peter that God was not a respecter of persons based on their nations of origin or any other such criterion. By the reckoning or standards of the Jewish Christians, the people gathered in Cornelius house were not qualified for salvation and so could not possibly receive the baptism of the Holy Spirit which was for the saved. However, God demonstrated that He had qualified them by grace.

The same applies to you. What is that height in life that you see yourself as not having the pedigree to rise to. The good news is that you have been qualified by grace.

Ephesians 2:3-10 (AMP)

3 Among these (unbelievers) we all once
    lived in the passions of our flesh
    (our behaviour governed by the
    sinful self), indulging the
    desires of human nature (without
    the Holy Spirit) and (the impulses) of the
    (sinful) mind. We were, by nature,
    children (under the sentence) of
    (God's) wrath, just like the rest

(of mankind).

4 But God, being (so very) rich in mercy,
   because of His great and wonderful love
   with which He loved us,

5 even when we were (spiritually) dead and
   separated from Him because of our sins,
   He made us (spiritually) alive together
   with Christ (for by His grace – His
   undeserved favour and mercy - you
   have been saved from God's judgment).

6 And He raised us up together with Him
   (when we believed), and seated us with
   Him in the heavenly places, (because we
   are) in Christ Jesus,

7 (and He did this) so that in the ages to
   come He might (clearly) show the
   immeasurable and unsurpassed
   RICHES OF HIS GRACE
   in (His) kindness toward us in
   Christ Jesus (by providing for
   our redemption).

8 For it is by grace (God's remarkable
   compassion and favour drawing
   you to Christ) that you have

been saved (actually delivered from
judgment and given eternal life)
through faith. And this (salvation) is
not of yourselves (not through your own
effort), but it is the underserved,
gracious) gift of God;

9   not as a result of (your) works (nor your
attempts to keep the Law), so that no one
will (be able to) boast or take credit in any
way (for his salvation).

10 For we are His workmanship
(His own master work, a work of art),
created in Christ Jesus (reborn from
above – spiritually transformed, renewed,
ready to be used) for good works, which
God prepared (for us) beforehand
(taking paths which He set), so that
we would walk in them (living the good
life which He prearranged and
made ready for us).

By grace, God has qualified you to do the
good works that He predestined. By grace, He
has qualified you to live the good life that He
prearranged and made ready for you to live. This

is not to say that life is a bed of roses. That God has prearranged and made ready a good life for you to live does not translate into you having a smooth sail all the way. However, it does translate into God having taken all the challenges you have met and will ever meet into consideration.

1 Corinthians 10:13 (NIV)

13 No temptation has seized you except what
is common to man. And God is faithful;
he will not let you be tempted beyond
what you can bear. But when you
are tempted, he will also provide a
way out so that you can stand up under it.

For every challenge, obstacle, roadblock, etc., you will ever encounter, God has made grace (in this case, enabling power) available to you to overcome same.

Psalm 37: 25

25   I have been young, and now am old;
yet I have not seen the righteous
forsaken, nor his descendants
begging bread.

In Psalm 37:25, David, the Psalmist, was not talking of the life of the righteous in terms of its parts but of the whole. David himself had suffered/endured lack and scarcity. He had encountered several challenges. Like we saw earlier in Chapter 7 of this book, he sent to Nabal requesting for food for himself and his men (1 Sam. 25:5-8). Apparently, they could do with more food, especially considering that they were in the wilderness - the Wilderness of Paran.

In 1 Samuel 30:1-2, Amalekites invaded Ziklag, where David and his men were staying, burnt the place with fire and

> **Looking at the WHOLE story of the life of a righteous man, it would be evident that he had not been forsaken.**

carried away their wives, sons and daughters captive. This happened in the absence of David and his men. They had accompanied Achish, king of Gath, to the battlefield, as the Philistines assembled to fight with Israel. It was on their return, not having been allowed to fight alongside the Philistines by the princes of the Philistines who distrusted David, that they met a burnt Ziklag.

Therefore, David knew that there could be times in the life of the righteous that it could look as if he had been forsaken by God. He was saying that, however, looking at the WHOLE story of the life of a righteous man, it would be evident that he had not been forsaken. The whole story of your life will declare that God did not forsake you.The whole story of your life will display how God dealt with you on the basis of grace and qualified you to reach your destiny by same.

Looking at parts of the life of Joseph, he looked forsaken. His pit, Potiphar's house, and prison experiences portrayed a young man whose life was full of anguish and sorrow. However, his palace experience changed all that and re-sounded the truth of Psalm 37:25.

If the nationality/nationalities of Cornelius and the people gathered in his house did not stop them from getting baptised in the Holy Ghost, you can be sure that your nation, town, village, household and family of origin cannot stop you from entering into what God has prepared for you.

Ephesians 2:11-13, 17-18

11 Therefore remember that you, once
Gentiles in the flesh – who are called
Uncircumcision by what is called the
Circumcision made in the flesh by hands –

12 that at that time you were without Christ,
being aliens from the commonwealth
of Israel and strangers from the covenants
of promise, having no hope and without
God in this world.

13 But now in Christ Jesus you who once
were afar off have been brought near by
the blood of Jesus.

17 And He came and preached peace to you
who were afar off and to those who
were near.

18 For through Him we both have access
by one Spirit to the Father.

If you have access (Vs. 18) to the Father, you can be certain that you have access to the desires of your heart. You have access to the good

If you have access to the Father, you can be certain that you have access to the desires of your heart.

life that God has prearranged for you to live. You have been qualified by grace. That is to say that you have been qualified by Christ. Christ is grace Personified.

Colossians 1:12-13

12 giving thanks to the Father WHO HAS QUALIFIED US to be partakers of the saints in the light.

13 He has delivered us from the power of darkness and conveyed us into the kingdom of the Son of His love.

It was, therefore, the deliverance from the power of darkness and the corresponding relocation into the kingdom of Christ ("the Son of His love") that made for our qualification. These were acts of grace since we were, by our nature and actions, supposed to be in bondage to the devil, and to have our dwelling in his (the devil's) kingdom. By grace, however, God qualified us to become partakers of what He had, having brought us into His family.

Christ is grace Personified.

2 Corinthians 3:5-6

5   Not that we are sufficient of ourselves to think of anything as being from ourselves, but our sufficiency is from God,

6   who also made us sufficient as ministers of the new covenant, not of the letter but of the Spirit, for the letter kills, but the Spirit gives life.

Here, Paul compares and contrasts the covenant God established through Moses with the new covenant He established through Christ. Though Moses complained of lack of competence and Pharaoh was unwilling to release the Israelites, God made Moses competent both in terms of ability and authority. Paul, therefore, argues that, in this same way, God now, by His Spirit, makes believers competent in both ability and authority to serve as "ministers of the new covenant."

> **If God, by the covenant He made with Moses, qualified him to carry out God's assignment for him (Moses), by the new covenant, God has much more qualified you to fulfil every assignment He has for you in life.**

If God, by the covenant He made with Moses, qualified him to carry out God's assignment for him (Moses), you can be sure that, by the new covenant, which is better than the former, and has better promises (Heb. 8:6), God has much more qualified you to fulfil every assignment He has for you in life. That is to say that God has also qualified you to partake of everything you need for every such assignment.

BETTER THAN BETHESDA

John 5:2-4

2   Now there is in Jerusalem by the Sheep
    Gate a pool, which is called in Hebrew,
    Bethesda, having five porches.

3   In these lay a great multitude of sick
    people, blind, lame, paralyzed, waiting
    for the moving of the water.

4   For an angel went down at a certain time
    into the pool and stirred up the water;
    then whoever stepped in first, after the
    stirring of the water, was made well
    of whatever disease he had.

A porch is a built-out roofed doorway to a building, i.e. a doorway with a canopy. The pool of Bethesda had five porches or doorways leading to it. Since the number five symbolises grace, you could day that the pool of Bethesda was a place of the operation of God's grace.

I stated at the beginning of this chapter that with God as grace Personified, grace has always been. It was, however, with the coming of the dispensation of grace, which the death of Christ ushered us into, that man again (since his fall) began to enjoy God's grace to the extent that we do now. Christ Himself lived under the dispensation of law since a testament (or will) can only come into effect after the death of the testator (Heb. 9:16-17). It was, therefore, the death of Christ, the Testator of the New Will (or Covenant) of grace that made the covenant effective. The 'operation of grace' at the pool of Bethesda, therefore, took place under the dispensation of law.

A look at the differences between what grace offers us now (you could say what obtains presently at the 'porches' of grace) and what obtained at Bethesda will help your understanding of the riches of God's grace:

(1) There is no ritualistic waiting under the 'porches' of grace.

*At Bethesda: "In these lay a great multitude of sick people, blind, lame paralysed, WAITING FOR THE MOVING OF THE WATER" (Jn. 5:3).

- Now, you can receive from God at any time. God is not hindered by any protocol from blessing you.

(2) There is no competition under the 'porches' of grace.

*At Bethesda: "For an angel went down at a certain time into the pool and stirred the water; then WHOEVER STEPPED IN FIRST, after the stirring of the water, WAS MADE WELL of whatever disease he had." (Jn. 5:4).

- Now, nobody's blessing can stop any other person's. Everybody can receive from God, even if needed/desired at the same time.

(3) Everyone that passes through the

'porches' of grace is made whole.

*At Bethesda: "For an angel went down at a certain time into the pool and stirred up the water; then WHOEVER stepped in first, after the stirring of the water, was made well of whatever disease he had" (Jn. 5:4).

Now, there is more than enough for everyone, no matter the number.

(4) You do not need man at the 'porches' of grace.

*At Bethesda: "The sick man answered Him, 'Sir, I HAVE NO MAN to put me into the pool when the water is stirred up; but while I am coming, another steps down before me' " (Jn. 5:7).

- Now, God is all you need. With Him, all things are possible. Any help you receive that is not God-inspired will not produce the required result.

(5) There is no legalism (observation of Sabbath, etc.) at the 'porches' of grace.

*At Bethesda: "The Jews therefore said to

him who was cured, 'It is the Sabbath; IT IS NOT LAWFUL for you to carry your bed' " (Jn. 5:10).

- Now, every day is for you a day of God's favour, salvation and promotion. You should be glad and rejoice each day.

(6)   The 'pool' of grace is always in motion. It does not need to be stirred up by an angel or any other being/thing.

*At Bethesda: "FOR AN ANGEL WENT DOWN AT A CERTAIN TIME INTO THE POOL AND STIRRED UP THE WATER; ... (Jn. 5:4).

- Now, you are the one to 'press into', and profit from the 'already stirred up pool of grace'.

(7)   The 'pool' of grace is a place of complete stories. God is not a God of half measures.

*At Bethesda: "But the one who was healed DID NOT KNOW who it was, for Jesus had withdrawn, a multitude being in that place. Afterward Jesus found him in the temple, and said to him, 'See, you have been made well. Sin no more, lest a worse thing come upon you.' The man departed and told the Jews that it was Jesus who had made him well" (Jn. 5:13-15).

- God always finishes what He begins (Phil. 1:6; Is. 34:16). As you hold unto Him, He will empower you to reach your destiny.

(8)   Jesus is the visibly glorified Lord at the 'pool' of grace.

At Bethesda: "But the one who was healed DID NOT KNOW WHO IT WAS, for Jesus had withdrawn, a multitude being in that place" (Jn. 5:13).

-    Everything about you should bring glory to God. Christ and His doings must be on continual display in your life.

As desirable as the riches of Bethesda were to a great number of people, the riches of God's grace which are available to us today are by far superior.

YOU HAVE TO GROW IN GRACE

2 Peter 1:2-11

2   Grace and peace be multiplied to you in the knowledge of God and of Jesus our Lord,

3   as His divine power has given to us all things that pertain to life and godliness, through the knowledge of Him who called us by glory and virtue,

4   by which have been given to us great and precious promises, that through these you may be partakers of the divine nature, having escaped the corruption that is in the world through lust.

5   But also for this very reason, giving all diligence, add to your faith virtue, to virtue knowledge,

6   to knowledge self-control, to self-control perseverance, to self-control perseverance, to perseverance godliness,

7   to godliness brotherly kindness, and to brotherly kindness love.

8   For if these things are yours and

abound, you will be neither barren
nor unfruitful in the knowledge of
our Lord Jesus Christ.

9   For he who lacks these things is
shortsighted, even to blindness, and has
forgotten that he was cleansed from
his old sins.

10 Therefore, brethren, be even more diligent
to make your call and election sure, for if
you do these things you will never stumble;

11 for so an entrance will be supplied to
you abundantly into the everlasting
kingdom of our Lord and Saviour
Jesus Christ.

To grow in grace is to grow in Christ-likedness.
Christ, like I said earlier, is grace Personified,
and so to grow in grace is to
become more like Him. To

To grow in grace is to grow in Christ-likedness.

grow in grace, therefore, is to
mature as a Christian. 2 Peter
3:18 says we should "grow in
the grace and knowledge of our Lord and Saviour
Jesus Christ."

We were saved by grace through faith (Eph. 2:8), and also, we develop and mature by grace. Grace (meaning God's unmerited favour), of its own, does not increase. It also does not decrease. But we can grow in our understanding and appreciation of it. As we do so, we will become more like Him.

1 Peter 2:21-24

21 For to this you were called, because Christ also suffered for us, leaving us an example, that you should FOLLOW HIS STEPS:

22 "Who committed no sin, nor was deceit found in His mouth";

23 who, when He was reviled, did not revile in return; when He suffered, He did not threaten, but committed Himself to Him who judges righteously;

24 who Himself bore our sins in His own body on the tree, that we, having died to sins, might live for righteousness – by whose stripes you were healed.

The number one priority of every right-thinking

person should be to make heaven. While it is wonderful to enjoy all of the godly goodies that abound in this world, this must be done on the way to heaven. To sacrifice eternity in God's presence on the altar of anything is foolishness of the highest order. Jesus asked, "For what profit is it to a man if he gains the whole world, and loses his own soul? Or what will a man give in exchange for his soul?" (Matthew 16:26).

> **The number one priority of every right-thinking person should be to make heaven.**

The way to heaven is the way of His steps. The way to heaven is the way Jesus took to return there. It is the way of purity; the way of holy living.

God's designed destiny for you is becoming all that He created you to be, and more importantly, arriving heaven at the end of your sojourn on the earth to live with God eternally. Anything short of this amounts to not fulfilling destiny. Peter (in 1 Pet. 2:22) captured the two basic elements of the steps of Jesus:

(1)   He committed no sin.
(2)   No deceit was found in His mouth.

The two elements are clearly related since the absence of deceit in a manifestation of holiness or living above sin. However, they are also distinct, viewed closely. The first element emphasises how He lived, i.e. His own conduct/comportment. The second is about how He provided guidance to others to live like Him.

Having told his readers in Verse 21 that they were called to patient endurance of injustice, in verse 23, Peter goes on to show how Jesus demonstrated the same. In doing this, a sinless Jesus was crucified, and there on the cross, He bore our sins in His body. Peter pointed out that Jesus did this so that we might die to sins and live for righteousness (Verse 24).

When your steps are aligned with the steps of Jesus, you are invariably living for righteousness. That way, your steps will be heading to your God-designed destiny. Your steps will also be heading to heaven.

With every new day, you should strive to be more like God.

God's children should pursue graciousness. With every new day, you should strive to be more like God. As you keep receiving and enjoying His grace, you should also become more and more gracious.

Titus 2:11-13 (AMP)

11 For the (remarkable, undeserved) grace of God that brings salvation has appeared to all men.

12 It teaches us to reject ungodliness and worldly (immoral) desires and to live sensible, upright, and godly lives (lives with A PURPOSE THAT REFLECT SPIRITUAL MATURITY) in this present age,

13 awaiting and confidently expecting the (fulfilment of our) blessed hope and the glorious appearing of our great God and Saviour, Christ Jesus,

Very clearly, therefore, grace, the unmerited/undeserved favour of God, teaches us to live godly lives. It instructs us to live lives which reflect

Even though we are living in the dispensation of grace, it is only as we live godly lives that we can confidently look forward to the Second Coming of Christ.

spiritual maturity. Grace is not a licence to sinfulness: "... Shall we continue in sin that grace may abound?" (Rom. 6:1). It is not a ticket to ungodliness. Even though we are living in (and enjoying) the dispensation of grace, it is only as we live godly lives that we can confidently look forward to the Second Coming of Christ.

Paul, writing to Roman believers, said, "But now having become slaves of God, you have your fruit to holiness, and the end, everlasting life" (Rom. 6:22).

Everlasting life is not only a present reality for believers: "And this is eternal life, that they may know You, the only true God, and Jesus Christ whom You have sent" (Jn. 17:3). It is also a future hope/destination. And the way to that future hope/destination is holiness.

Of course, that destination can only be reached

in Christ, i.e. by believers. But the believers have to 'enslave' themselves to righteousness through obedience. Enslavement to sin will result in spiritual death: "Do you not know that to whom you present yourselves slaves to obey, you are that one's slaves whom you obey, whether of SIN LEADING TO DEATH, or of obedience leading to righteousness?" (Rom. 6:16). "For the wages of SIN IS DEATH, but the gift of God is eternal life in Christ Jesus our Lord" (Rom. 6:23). Paul instructed Titus to constantly affirm that believers "should be careful to maintain good works" (Titus 3:8).

The word, 'righteousness,' has two definitions in the Bible, with the context in which it is used determining which definition is applicable. It means 'right standing': "... Abraham believed God and it was accounted to him for righteousness" (Rom. 4:3). It also means 'good or right works': "..., let no one deceive you. He who practices righteousness is righteous, just as He is righteous" (1 Jn. 3:7). The first is a gift (from God); the second is not – it is 'lived out'.

It is also important to know that salvation could

be said to be in three phases. There is the former salvation, which is of the spirit of man: "... by grace you have been saved through faith,..." (Eph. 2:8). "..., that which is born of the Spirit is spirit" (Jn. 3:6). There is the present salvation, which involves the soul: "...., work out your own salvation with fear and trembling" (Phil. 2:12). "..., be transformed by the renewing of your mind, ..." (Rom. 12:2). And there is the latter salvation, which will involve the body. "…. he who endures to the end shall be saved" (Mtt. 24:13). "For this corruptible must put on incorruption, and this mortal must put on immortality" (1 Cor. 15:53).

These three phases constitute the complete salvation package. No wonder Paul prayed, "Now may the God of peace Himself sanctify you completely; and may your whole spirit, soul, and body be preserved blameless at the coming of our Lord Jesus Christ" (1 Thess. 5:23). Again, like Ephesians 2:8 says, that of the spirit is "the gift of God."

In the light of these assertions (and others in the Bible), and knowing that Scriptures cannot contradict themselves, it is clear that genuine salvation is entirely of God; is the product of His grace, and that it results, inevitably, in a life of good works. You are not saved by good works, but you are definitely saved unto (or for) good works. The new creation is God's making, with man having nothing to do with it; your salvation having been ordained by God from eternity. The resulting good works are also empowered by God: "God is working in you, giving you the desire and the power to do what pleases him" (Phil. 2:13, NLT).

Though our gracious God does not condemn the sinner, He does not condone sin; and, definitely, cannot commend it. After dismissing the accusers of the woman caught in the act of adultery, Jesus said to her, "Neither do I condemn you; go and sin no more" (John 8:11). In the words of Pastor Poju Oyemade, "Grace is not just about no longer being under condemnation, but it's also about living the 'In-Christed' life in which life and immortality are made manifest in us. It is about understanding

"The Spirit can never produce a life which is inferior to that which power and might achieved."

how to live the new life we have received from God. It's not through power and might but by the Spirit. The Spirit can never produce a life which is inferior to that which power and might achieved."

Paul told King Agrippa that he "declared first to those in Damascus and in Jerusalem and throughout all the region of Judea, and then to the Gentiles, that they should repent, turn to God, and do WORKS BEFITTING REPENTANCE" (Acts 26:20). So, there are works that befit repentance. There is a lifestyle that gives credence to being a child of God.

If you say you are a child of God, then your walk must agree with that talk.

Several Scriptures make it clear that there is THE WALK THAT VALIDATES THE TALK. If you say you are a child of God, then your walk must agree with that talk. Somebody said, "What you are doing is so loud I can't hear what you are saying."

Consider the following Scriptures:

1 John 1:5-6

5   This is the message which we have heard
from Him and declare to you, that God
is light and in Him is no darkness at all.

6   IF WE SAY we have fellowship with Him,
and walk in darkness, we lie and do not
practice the truth.

'To walk', in Greek, is 'peripateo' – to walk around;
a style of life.

1 John 1:8-9

8   IF WE SAY we have no sin, we deceive
ourselves, and the truth is not in us.

9   If we confess our sins, He is faithful and
just to forgive us our sins and cleanse us
from all unrighteousness.

The Bible, evidently, does not teach sinless
perfection. On the contrary, it teaches that even
the most mature; most godly Christian is still
susceptible to sin. What 1John 8-9 teach is that
one of the greatest evidences that a person is
born again; that a person is truly a child of God,
is that he will be sensitive to the sin in his life

and will be led to repentance and confession of that sin.

1 John 2:3-4

3   Now by this we know that we know Him,
    if we keep His commandments.

4   HE WHO SAYS, "I know Him," and does
    not keep His commandments, is a liar,
    and the truth is not in him.

Again, this is a reference, not to sinless perfection, but to a lifestyle of obedience to God and His Word. When you have a new relationship with God, you will have a new relationship with His commands. You will also have a new attitude to sin – that of declining interest in it.

1 John 2:6

6   HE WHO SAYS he abides in Him ought
    himself also to walk just as He walked.

What is the great desire of your heart? As a child of God, you should desire to put your foot in His footprints.

1 John 2:9

9   HE WHO SAYS he is in the light, and
     hates his brother, is in darkness until now.

If you say that you know God and yet you do not
love other believers in real and practical ways,
and desire fellowship with them, your claim is
questionable.

1 John 2:15

15 Do not love the world or the things in the
     world. If anyone loves the world, the love
     of the Father is not in him.

The 'world' here refers to everything in this fallen
age that contradicts the attributes and will of
God. If you still have UNRESTRAINED love for
the things that nailed your supposed Master
to the cross, you surely do not love Him. Stop
claiming to be a believer.

1 John 2:22-23

22 Who is a liar but he who denies that
    Jesus is the Christ? He is anti-Christ who
    denies the Father and the Son.

23 Whoever denies the Son does not have the Father either; he who acknowledges the Son has the Father also.

The true Christian will embrace the fullness of the Person of Jesus Christ. You must believe in, receive, and embrace the fullness of His Person, not only as Saviour, but also as Lord.

1 John 2:29

29 If you know that He is righteous, you know that everyone that practices righteousness is born of Him.

As earlier said, aside from meaning right standing with God, righteousness also means conforming to the nature and law of God. Do you practice righteousness? Are you practicing God's law; God's wisdom; God's Word; God's precepts? Is that a practice in your life?

In Matthew 7:23, Jesus said, "Depart from me, you who practice lawlessness." There are many who claim to be Christ's disciples and yet live as if God never gave them instructions to follow. Inasmuch as a legalism is 'death', however, the

Bible instructs us on how we should live.

1 John 3:3 says, "And everyone that has this hope in Him purifies himself, just as He is pure." Hear this: Everyone that believes in the Second Coming of Jesus Christ, and is looking forward to it, must purify himself. Not only has God sanctified us in Christ; He also calls us to strive to be holy. Not to struggle to be holy, but to align our lives with His Word in a determination to live lives worthy of our profession.

The journey from Jacob to Israel was one of continued growth in grace. It was one of impressive, continued spiritual maturation. At the beginning, we saw a young man whose major concern was to please himself; whose steps were guided by selfish ambition. By the end, we saw a man who only concern was to advance the cause of the God of his fathers; whose steps were ordered by God-given-vision.

You too can make up your mind to grow continuously in grace. You must commit yourself to the advancement of God's cause; God's kingdom. Your steps must be ordered by God and His vision for you.

I see you living out completely God's intention for creating you. I see you getting to the very end of your 'purposeway'. You will reach your destiny!

OTHER BOOKS BY THE SAME AUTHOR

In His first communication with the peak of His creation. God commissions man to "be fruitful, and multiply, replenish the earth, subdue it and have dominion over it" (Genesis 1:28).

What are the demands and responsibilities placed on man by this commission? What are man's benefits therefrom? And who are the people that are "qualified" to carry out the said commission?

In this highly incisive, inspiring and informative book, Pastor Chudi Egbuonu makes a convincing case of why and how the believer must bestride his heavenly Father's creation like a colossus.

COMMISSIONED TO CONQUER is meant to make you hate mediocrity with everything in you and provoke you to begin to conform to your Creator's plan and purpose for you - one of all-round excellence.

ISBN 978-37070-9-4

- The raison d'etre of the New Birth was the failure of the Old Birth.
- Christianity is not synonymous with mediocrity.
- Adequate provisions have been made to enable the believer to excel in life.
- Trials and temptations make for tastier triumphs and testimonies.
- Facts change but truth is constant. The fact of what you are today does not change the truth of who you are in Christ.
- Calvary restored the believer to the Garden of Eden.
- The New Birth is all-encompassing – your salvation ticket covers all the meals on your trip to heaven.
- The believer has a glorious destiny in God. Every new day brings him closer to that destiny.

With these truths and others, THE EXCELLENCY OF THE NEW BIRTH strives to make the believer appreciate the WHOLESOME PROMOTION he received by getting born-again, and provoke him to appropriate and live same.

ISBN 978-37070-6-X

YOU CAN BE THE NEXT SECCESS STORY strives to show you how very much within your reach success really is. It is a simple, matter-of-fact, step-by-step approach to actualizing your dream of success in life. This book will defeat hopelessness, inferiority complex, indecisiveness and every other success-repellent in you, and stimulate you to go for success like you have never done.

YOU CAN BE THE NEXT SUCCESS STORY shows you that...
- Success is conceived in the heart – in the *womb* of the heart.
- All that you need to become a success story is in, and with you right now.
- In God's design of you, He provided you with every necessary faculty, every necessary facility and every necessary function that you need to succeed.
- You must put in everything you have and know into the writing of your success story.

ISBN 978-37070-0-6

- The wilderness should be a place for meditation; a place of reflection.
- It should be a place of meaningful communication with God.
- The wilderness should be a time of addition, not subtraction; profit, not loss; increase, not decrease; life, not death.
- It should be a time of re-alignment of forces and strategies; a time of re-focusing, re-dedication and re-adjustment.
- It should be a time to retrospection and introspection.
- The wilderness should be a time of re-ordering of priorities; a time of re-appraisal of objectives; a time of re-direction and re-orientation.
- You were neither ordained to die in any wilderness nor to spend forty years in it.
- In God's Word are the principles and pattern to walk through any wilderness with affordable effort and ease, and to come out of it in good time.

These principles and pattern are the POWER you need TO WADE THROUGH YOUR WILDERNESS.

ISBN 978-37070-7-0

THE AUTHOR

Pastor Chudi Egbuonu is the Senior Pastor of Purposeway Christian Centre, Abuja - Nigeria, a vibrant local assembly with the mandate of 'Defining Direction, Delivering Destiny'.

He is also the President of Pastureland Resources, a multi-faceted Christian media organisation that has the printed page as its major thrust.

Pastor Chudi is a powerful preacher and anointed teacher with proven signs in ministry. He has ministered God's word extensively within and outside Nigeria,

With a background in architecture, he holds other qualifications including a Master of Science Degree in project management from the University of Salford, Manchester.

An accomplished author, he has written other books including **The Excellency of the New Birth, Commissioned to Conquer, Power to Wade through your Wilderness,** and **You can be next Success Story.**

He is married to Rosebud, and they are blessed with four lovely children - Hephzibah, Carmela, Jedidiah and Enoch.

www.ingramcontent.com/pod-product-compliance
Lightning Source LLC
Chambersburg PA
CBHW020123180726
47992CB00020B/1870